How Do You and Your Love Partner Fit?

Cuing In

The Secure/Secure Couple

—

Running To, Running From

The Secure/Avoidant Couple

—

The Owl and the Hummingbird

The Secure/Ambivalent Couple

—

Ships That Pass in the Night

The Avoidant/Avoidant Couple

—

Cool in the Heart of a Storm

The Avoidant/Ambivalent Couple

—

All Over the Emotional Map

The Ambivalent/Ambivalent Couple

Couple Fits

How to Live with the Person You Love

Evelyn S. Cohen, M.S., and Sheila A. Rogovin, Ph.D.,
with Andrea Thompson

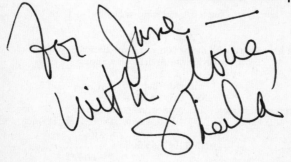

For Jane —
with love
Sheila

A Perigee Book

A Perigee Book
Published by The Berkley Publishing Group
A division of Penguin Putnam Inc.
375 Hudson Street
New York, New York 10014

First edition: January 2000

Published simultaneously in Canada.

The Penguin Putnam Inc. World Wide Web site address is
http://www.penguinputnam.com

Library of Congress Cataloging-in-Publication Data

Cohen, Evelyn S.
Couple fits : how to live with the person you love / Evelyn S. Cohen and Sheila
A. Rogovin with Andrea Thompson
p.   cm.
Includes index.
ISBN 0-399-52573-4
1. Interpersonal relations.   2. Man-woman relationships.   3. Couples
4. Attachment behavior   5. Love.   I. Rogovin, Sheila A. (Sheila Anne) 1931–
II. Thompson, Andrea.   III. Title.
HM1106.C63 2000
306.7—dc21   99-046782
                                                        CIP

Printed in the United States of America

10   9   8   7   6   5   4   3   2   1

For Emily, Julia, Lily, and David, who will help shape and influence the romantic climate of the future.

SAR

For RGC, my partner in a lifelong intimate journey.

ESC

Contents

Preface

MAYBE you've been married to or living with your partner for years, or for just a few months.

Maybe you're dating someone, things look serious, and you're wondering whether you *should* make a more serious commitment.

Or you're in a committed relationship that's contained more stress than happiness lately.

Or you and your partner are basically content, but you suspect you could be even more so. Life feels a little flat these days.

You may want to jump-start a stalled relationship, find ways to have fewer fights, work out issues before they become problems, or avoid making the mistakes you think your parents made. Or possibly you're in the midst of a full-blown crisis. Whatever your relationship looks like, here's what we know about you: If you have bought *Couple Fits*, or the title has caught your attention in the bookstore and you're thumbing through it right now, you want to preserve and improve your love life!

You have a lot of company. A couple of decades ago many adults held a me-first attitude that was reflected in a number of popular books at the time: Unhappy with your partner? Leave and find a better life for yourself.

Not any more. The couples we are seeing these days want to stay together. They want to fix what's wrong, heal the wounds, and recapture the good feelings they used to enjoy. The lessons of recent years point to the good sense of those wishes. Couples who ignore early problems are especially likely to divorce later. Broken homes are hard on kids. No-fault divorce has had devastatingly negative effects. "Mismanaged conflict" between couples, according to a large recent study, predicts poor physical and mental health and decreased work productivity. Sexually transmitted diseases have people wary. So yes, staying together makes a lot of sense.

Here's something else we know about you: You *can* find the greater stability, joy, and comfort in your relationship that you yearn for. You *can* improve your love life. We know, because we've helped hundreds of couples do just that. We're going to show you how.

"You and I are going to be a chapter in her book!" said a woman in one of our counseling sessions recently, turning to her husband. Then, although we had indicated nothing along those lines, she said to us, "You are writing a book, aren't you? You should. This is great stuff!"

We think it's great stuff too. And we know it works.

In *Couple Fits*, we will introduce you to attachment style, a most dynamic way of understanding what's happening in your marriage or intimate relationship: why with all the love in the world, you and your partner are so often at loggerheads, or you're frequently down in the dumps, or he never seems to understand what you're talking about. And you will learn how to improve that picture.

Of the many efforts to understand why lovers run into difficulties, we believe that attachment style offers the most integrated view—and a most useful tool for effecting change. Mapped out decades ago as a way of explaining childhood development, attachment theory applied to adult love relationships and marriage is a way of interpreting human behavior that suggests concrete and practical measures by which couples can be a whole lot happier and more comfortable. It's the core of what we do as therapists, the way we come at the problems those two people sitting on the couch in front of us are struggling with.

In the course of counseling hundreds of couples, we've been able to identify *in every single case* the dominant style that propels each partner to act in certain ways. And we have seen again and again that once each can recognize and make sense of their attachment patterns, life improves and the difficulties that brought them in for help are infinitely more manageable. They learn to leave the battles outside the door, and make the relationship an oasis of comfort.

In fact, if even only *one* partner "gets it," life improves!

Couples we work with are hooked on this new way of understanding each other, and we're confident that after reading *Couple Fits*, you will be too. It is both simple and profound. And you may find it will, happily, change your life.

In the following chapters, we'll help you plumb the emotional currents that flow between you and your partner. You will come to recognize the squabbles or silences, the disappointments or resentments, the stalemates or misunderstandings as the products of attachment styles. And the good news is that it is well within your power to bring those styles into better harmony.

You'll learn how to talk to your partner more clearly about what you want and need, and how to encourage him or her to do the same.

You'll learn to "read" arguments correctly, by recognizing the underlying issues at stake.

You'll become less likely to misinterpret each other's motivations; one partner's actions will not necessarily signify a personal attack on the other.

You'll get better at giving negative feedback, and find that disagreements don't need to escalate into major fights.

And the whole level of resentment and frustration will go down. You will accommodate each other's differences more easily. You'll experience a greater degree of charity and compassion. Life will become sweeter!

Here's the beauty of what you're about to learn in *Couple Fits*: There is nothing right or wrong, good or bad, about any of these three types. Attachment style is as much a part of us as being brown-eyed or blue-eyed, left-handed or right-handed. It won't be *changed*, but it can be understood and used to promote—in fact, to guarantee—a smoother, happier road.

A word about what this book will not do for you:

You will not learn in these pages whom you ought to choose as your life's partner. Many influences, as we all know, come into play to bring two people together—romance, admiration, passion, money, background, religion, idealization. In all our counseling work with hundreds of couples, we have found no correlation between whom one picks and attachment style. Love has nothing to do with attachment style. You may have fallen for a know-it-all egotist, or a dreamy artist, or an individual who in one way or another will always be "difficult."

Love is love.

But you *will* learn how to get along with that partner better. You *will* see what you would be wise to do if you want this relationship to work. We'll show you where you must set limits and encourage change, and where you must accept and accommodate.

A word about the authors: We are both marriage and family therapists, with a combined fifty years' experience between us. Evelyn's practice is based in New York City; Sheila's is in Chevy Chase, Maryland. Over the years, we've been each other's best consultant and sounding board, and we approach our counseling work from the same point of view.

Consequently, we've found it professionally comfortable and literarily sensible to meld ourselves into one, so to speak, for ease in presenting the ideas in *Couple Fits*. So, for example, we'll refer to "our office" or "our client." The stories of couples and individuals that make up the core of this book are ones we've plucked from our case experiences, although we've altered the specifics to protect their anonymity.

That shared point of view includes this simple bias: In the absence of physical abuse or other factors that make a relationship truly untenable, we believe two people who came together in love should stay together. Since you've decided to read this book, we're assuming that's your bias too. It's a good one.

Now let us show you how to make it happen.

Acknowledgments

WE are grateful to the many people who have contributed to our understanding of attachment theory and to the various steps along the path to book publication.

Our children and husbands offered their constant and loving support, and perceptive insights as well. Our good friend Nick Lyons generously gave both encouragement and professional commentary during the beginning stages of this work; Janet Laffey and Marion Porter were of great help in preparing the early drafts. Many close friends and colleagues offered, without reservation, their personal and professional experiences and critiques. Our thanks to them all.

From the studies of John Bowlby, Robert Fairbairn, Mary Ainsworth, Mary Main, Henry Dicks, Cindy Hazen, Philip Shaver and others, we have been able to conceptualize what we consider this most useful way for couples to understand their intimate relationships. We are grateful for that sound theoretical framework, which helped convince us that attachment theory offers a powerful and enduring option for the treatment of marital conflict.

We express our great appreciation to our agent, Stedman Mays, for his unswerving faith in and commitment to *Couple Fits*, and to our editor, John Duff, for believing in it in the first place.

PART I

Coming Together, Being Apart

CHAPTER 1

Ways of Connecting:
Introducing Attachment Theory

A man and woman—we'll call them Bill and Mary Smith—came to our office for help. After four contented years together, their marriage was shaky. Bill and Mary loved each other, they said; they just weren't liking each other much anymore, and they didn't seem to be able to talk without starting a fight.

Over the course of several sessions, we learned a lot about the Smiths. Like most newlyweds, these two had begun their marriage with a reservoir of goodwill, loving feelings, and high hopes. They enjoyed a lot of the same things, they said, like football, hiking, and going out to restaurants and movies. They disliked the same things, like Thai food, country music, and the Republican party. Back then, sex was frequent and satisfying. They worked hard, made nice money, and hoped to buy a house and start a family. Back then, they rarely argued about who should throw in a load of laundry or take the car for an oil change.

Despite these shared interests and compatible drives, Mary

and Bill were not carbon copies of each other. Mary tended to be emotional, voluble, and happiest when she was involved in all the details of her husband's life. Bill was laid back, a man who didn't enjoy initiating conversation and preferred to take care of business on his own. Bill, generally, was delighted that Mary showed so much interest in him and did most of the talking. Mary, generally, found that living with such a relaxed and apparently cool and confident partner made her feel reassured and calmer than she used to be.

These were two people seemingly meant to be together. But lately, life had thrown them a few curves, and the differences that had seemed complementary were causing them pain. The past several months had been a rocky patch for Bill, who lost his management job in a downsizing purge. Being unemployed, a new and corrosive experience for him, made Bill moody and restless. The Smiths weren't hurting for money, but tension between the two was thick and mounting. They were getting on each other's nerves.

Whenever Bill came home from a job interview, for example, Mary peppered him with questions before the door was even closed behind him. When he received a phone call, she hovered nearby, making little hand gestures in an effort to find out who was calling or to suggest what he should say. The more she hovered, the more he withdrew; his responses to her overtures and questions became more and more perfunctory. The more he withdrew, the more agitated and argumentative or sullen and hurt she became.

Mary started to perceive her husband's laid-back attitude as indifference to her. "It's like pulling teeth to get this guy to tell me the simplest thing," she said. Bill was too far away for her comfort.

Bill started to perceive his wife as intrusive and demanding; her interest felt to Bill like nagging. "I wish she'd just get off my back—or out of my face all the time," he said. Mary was too close for his comfort.

Often these days, spats over nothing much flared up between them. As Bill sat reading his newspaper one evening, Mary suddenly charged in from the kitchen and yanked the paper out of his hands. "You're not even reading that, are you?" she shouted. "You just like having a physical barrier up so you don't have to talk to me." Personalizing her partner's behavior, she took it as an attack on her. The next morning as they walked toward their car, which Mary had left on the street the night before, Bill had a comment to make about her parking job: "Did you pay off the guy to skip the parallel parking part of your driver's test? It's nothing short of a miracle that we still have a left fender." Angry at his partner for being perpetually in his face, he came up with an unrelated complaint and a bit of sarcasm to put her down.

Privately, each sometimes wondered whether the marriage had been such a great idea in the first place.

In this time of stress, Bill and Mary Smith were demonstrating different *attachment styles*, or different ways of behaving in order to stay comfortably close to (or distant from) each other. Bill pulls away from his partner and constrains his feelings, both to himself and to Mary. Trying to keep everything under wraps, he wishes Mary would settle down and leave him alone. Bill is *avoidant*.

Uncomfortable with closeness and intimacy, the avoidant's behavior is uninvolved and withholding. Emotionally distant relationships feel best to this individual, who believes that conflict should be averted at all costs.

Mary lets her feelings run away with her; she's either all over her partner, plucking at him for reassurance and connection, or silent and fuming ominously. Much of the time she connects with Bill by fighting with him, which only makes her more disquieted. Her darting-in/darting-out behaviors signal an anxious or *ambivalent* style.

The ambivalent feels unsure about the availability of others, and is very worried about being abandoned. This individual's relationships are typically feisty, characterized by a lot of arguing or a lot of needy loving.

Unless those styles could be reconciled, Mary and Bill were on a collision course.

Happily, we can report, that crash never happened; the marriage survived and then thrived. Bill will always be avoidant. Mary will always be ambivalent. Attachment styles don't go away. But two people can move toward a deeper understanding and acceptance of each other's style, and discover how to act in ways that do not threaten the heart of the relationship. For Mary and Bill, that meant adapting and putting into practice some of the reactions that typically characterize a *secure* style, one that allows for more open communication, more rational confrontation of issues, and eventual adjustment and moving on. They learned over time to identify each other's attachment patterns, make sense of them, and proceed to modify and renegotiate many ways they responded to each other. They recognized those elements of each one's style that had brought them happily together in the first place—Bill's relaxed, aloof manner and Mary's passionate, noisy manner—and could appreciate that such behavior was neither all good nor all bad. They learned how to forge a more successful couple fit.

Attachment styles have a simple function: They are the behaviors we all use to feel the greatest degree of emotional comfort and security in intimate interactions, most especially with a love partner.

Each of us acquires a particular style in infancy, as mother and baby give and receive comfort in their own unique ways, based on a combination of factors—baby's temperament, genetic wiring, and overall health; mom's temperament, child-raising beliefs, and psychological "baggage"; socioeconomic and other family characteristics, and so on. (We refer here and in the following chapter most often to mothers because, obviously, mother/child is the significant early pairing for the great majority of children. But an attachment style will evolve between a youngster and any primary caregiver or caregivers.)

Even before an infant is old enough to start toddling around on his own, he has developed a strategy for managing his most important relationship—with Mom, his first love object. He's learned how to handle his emotions—affection, anger, anxiety, fear—in ways that make him feel okay. He's worked out his first, most primitive and most powerful survival mechanism.

Like the baby bear in the old nursery rhyme, our youngster is determined that life be not too hot, not too cold, not too hard, not too soft, but just right. He wants to be attached to Mom in a way that feels close enough and distant enough. He doesn't want to be asked for more than he can give or expect more than he will receive. He wants to feel comfortable.

Much substantial research has revealed this surprising fact: Those most-comfortable behaviors can be clumped into just three patterns or primary attachment styles: *secure, avoidant,* and *ambivalent.* Our baby has learned to handle his emotions by dealing with them head on, or by denying and dodging them, or by feeling anxious and overwhelmed by them.

As that child grows up, his primary style sticks with him, functioning as his central organizing system for getting along with other people and the predominant way he identifies himself in relationships. But as he goes to school, makes friends, becomes an adult, gets a job, and in other ways moves ever outward and onward, he learns what works and what doesn't in the world at large. And what works best most of the time, he may discover, is essentially secure behavior—to be pleasantly responsive and adequately responsible, to take appropriate actions, to try to be tolerant and understanding, to face up to conflicts constructively, to not call people nasty names.

With classmates, pals, bosses, or co-workers, then, the avoidant's or the ambivalent's primary style is not always front and center. Distance, maturity, social graces, and workplace savvy all help her to accommodate to the life around her—to behave acceptably within the many interactions she encounters, showing her true attachment colors only in insignificant bits and pieces. A born avoidant, for example—an individual who's constitutionally uncomfortable expressing her needs, displaying emotions, or asking for help—may behave quite forthrightly on the job: acknowledging and working out differences, offering personal opinions, being confrontational when the occasion warrants. The dyed-in-the-wool ambivalent, whose instinct is to charge into battle, may be perfectly capable of keeping a lid on rash behavior at work.

Even the level-headed secure may be given to the occasional irrational outburst or head-in-the-sand reaction in the run-of-the-mill, day-to-day business of life. Indeed, any avoidant, ambivalent, or secure will display a sprinkling of behaviors from across the styles.

Then one day our grown-up falls in love. He joins forces with the person who will be his lover, best friend, partner, soul mate, spouse; he is once again linked to a principal attachment figure. Emotionally, it is as if he is back in the cradle. He feels, as he did when his life began, "I can cope with the world because I have you."

And he will tend to handle the emotions that flow between lovers according to the primary style he developed as an infant—by meeting, dodging, or being utterly overwhelmed by them. His partner, meanwhile, is doing the same. This is by no means necessarily a prescription for disaster. As two people figure out ways to handle conflicts, their attachment styles may work well together and even account for a lot of the juice between them.

But the path of any relationship, as we know, is never everlastingly smooth, and love does not conquer all. Stress comes from without (somebody loses a job, a baby is born, a child needs special help, somebody gets sick, somebody has an affair) or from within (one partner starts feeling ignored or senses that she and her lover have drifted apart or wonders why she isn't getting as much out of this union as she expected to). Then each partner's predominant attachment behavior surfaces in its purest form, with good or damaging results.

Listen to Bill and Mary Smith again, as they recalled some childhood memories.

Mary remembered her parents as being "preoccupied," caught up in their own interests and concerns. Her father was a professional illustrator, a naturalist, and an ardent fly-fisherman; her mother was an accomplished artist who sketched landscapes. When they went on outings to pursue those passions, Mary always longed to go with them. She would beg and plead, or throw an occasional temper tantrum, or promise to be good. Sometimes her parents gave in to her pleadings and took her with them; many times they didn't. Mary never knew when her requests would be heeded or why. Her parents' reactions seemed to be based on how they happened to be feeling that day, and had little to do with Mary's attempts to influence them.

Mary's mother alternated between over- and underinvolvement in her daughter's schoolwork. Mary remembered this incident: "When I was in fourth grade, we had to produce a drawing of some living creature. My mother made the drawing for me, a sketch of a butterfly with gorgeous wings that looked as if they were stained glass. I didn't want her to do this, but she told me I should say I made the picture. She said, 'You could do this yourself if you had more time,' although I knew that wasn't true. So I handed in the drawing, and the teacher raved about it and asked me how long it had taken. I had no idea so I said ten minutes. That night my mother was furious with me and said I had to go in the next day and say the drawing had actually taken me an hour. So I did that, feeling like everybody knew I was a total fraud."

During that same year, Mary struggled mightily with her arithmetic homework. Although her parents were aware of the hard time she was having, neither offered assistance.

Here's Bill: "My parents prized independence. They still do—they're kind of free thinkers, they don't follow the expected paths." Bill, the oldest of three siblings, was allowed a lot of latitude from an early age. He was never told when he had to be home from school, for example, and he spent many hours exploring in the woods around his home and amassing elaborate rock and leaf collections. Bill was often reminded he was "a big boy" and should keep an eye out for his younger brother and sister.

Bill said, "One of my mother's favorite expressions, if I started to tell her about some problem or something, was 'Cut to the solution.' Long-windedness is not encouraged in my family! My folks always conveyed the message that you don't dwell on what's happened—you figure out what to do and get going." This message, he thought, accounted for a lot of his proud and fiercely self-reliant nature.

Mealtimes were often quiet: "My mother and father are huge readers, and they always had a book going. Either of them or sometimes both would be reading during dinner. We could read too if we wanted to, and we had these little metal stands you could prop your book on." One evening, Bill remembered, he was happy to have his book up there in front of him. Still hurting from a friend's rejection earlier that day, he felt on the verge of tears, and didn't want the others to see his face.

From her parents' inconsistent reactions to her wishes and her need for support, we might guess Mary picked up early on a notion that she could do little to affect the behavior of others. She had to keep pressing to get her way, but her efforts to pull them to her or keep them a little further removed from her affairs sometimes worked and sometimes didn't.

From his parents' reluctance to put much store in the emotional side of life, Bill learned not to ask for or expect attention to his feelings. He adopted the belief that to succeed with others it was necessary to keep one's problems to oneself and take independent action to solve them.

We'll explore this intriguing matter of how attachment styles take root and grow a little more thoroughly in the next chapter.

CHAPTER 2

Three Styles and How They Grow

GET a bunch of mothers talking about their babies and you'll hear a bunch of different stories. This youngster was "fussy from day one," this one is "an easy baby, hardly ever cries," that one is "standoffish, doesn't like to be held for very long," and so on. If those babies could speak, they'd also report that mothers come in different varieties—one is right on the scene when baby needs some hugs and cuddles, another doesn't always come at a cry and likes to stick to a schedule about feeding, and so on.

As the mother/baby pair try to figure each other out, Mom is learning how to help her baby feel safe and protected, and the baby is learning how to get the comfort he needs when he needs it. All the cries, fussing, coos, gurgles, and smiles are signals that the baby uses to regulate his parent's reaction. And Mother, by responding, teaches her infant how to cause that reaction. Gradually these two negotiate a pattern—a way of keeping in touch at a satisfying distance—that seems to work for the both of them.

Now, get together a bunch of mothers, each of whom has more than one child, and each is likely to tell you that babies one and two were like night and day and baby three was something else entirely. To keep in touch and get what she wants, one child is a sulker, one makes a lot of noise and throws fits, and one is a little charmer who aims to please. It's the *interaction* between caregiver and one child that determines how the pattern works itself out. But however it does work itself out, the negotiating that starts at birth becomes set early in life. By the time she's roughly a year old, that youngster has developed a secure, avoidant, or ambivalent style.

In a nutshell, that's the basis of attachment theory, which for decades researchers have explored through various measures, most famously a now-classic study called the Strange Situation Test. Developed in the late 1960s by psychologist Mary Ainsworth, the Strange Situation engineers a little mini-drama that, theorists say, contains clues to the parent/child relationship that's already been established.

In the procedure, which lasts about twenty minutes, a one-year-old child and his parent (usually Mom) are brought into a playroom that's filled with appealing toys and given time to explore it together. After a while, a "stranger," part of the psychological team, enters the room. Parent, child, and stranger chat or play a bit, and then Mom leaves. The stranger tries to involve the child in play. A short time later, Mom returns. The whole episode is recorded on videotape.

From this simple set of circumstances, the psychological team, studying the tape, observes how the youngster handles a number of challenges: exploring a new place and interacting with his mother in a novel situation, meeting a stranger, using Mom to feel more comfortable with the stranger, separating from Mom, engaging with the stranger on his own, and finally—and most significantly—reuniting with Mom.

From those observations, the psychologists classify the youngster's behavior into one of three patterns—secure, avoidant, or ambivalent.

Here's how each child typically acts:

Secure Jenny. This child is a bit wary at first of this room she's never been in before. So she runs a little security check with her mom, looking at her and picking up signals that it's okay to proceed—this is a safe and friendly place—and pretty soon she's happily involved with some of those intriguing toys.

Jenny isn't especially bothered when the stranger enters, but she's not too happy when Mom goes out of the room, leaving her behind. She might register Mom's departure by searching for her and crying, or maybe by just becoming quiet and not so interested in the neat toys anymore. Perhaps she lets the stranger comfort her and entice her into a little playing.

Mom returns, and Jenny is delighted. She looks at Mom with a big smile. Maybe she runs over to her for a hug, maybe lets her pick her up for a little kiss. Soon she feels like playing again.

Avoidant Johnny. Johnny, apparently not bothered by the newness of the playroom, sets off exploring at once. He doesn't need to check with Mom to see whether the room is safe or to help him get adjusted to the novelty of the place. He'll get a little game going on his own or maybe want Mom to join in. Neither is he upset when the stranger comes in to join them.

When Mom leaves, Johnny doesn't protest or seem to register her going, and continues to play as he did before. He engages with the stranger as easily as with his parent.

When she comes back, Johnny mostly ignores his mother; in fact, he seems hardly to notice her presence. He avoids contact by walking away or shifting his posture to escape his mother's gaze.

Ambivalent Julie. This youngster is clearly unhappy over the unfamiliarity of the whole situation. She stays right by Mom, maybe clings to her leg, not able to overcome her distress enough to enjoy those tempting new toys. The stranger comes in and Julie sticks even closer to Mom.

When her mother leaves, Julie cries and cries, oblivious to the stranger's efforts to comfort and soothe her.

Mom returns, but their reunion doesn't seem to make Julie feel much better. Maybe she races to her, arms outstretched, but when Mom picks Julie up, she pushes Mom away, arching her back and struggling to be put down. Maybe she cries even louder. Maybe she tries to give her a punch. Julie doesn't know whether she's happy or sad to see Mom again.

And here, according to attachment theory, is why Jenny, Johnny, and Julie act in those separate ways, and how each is likely to display those learned responses as he or she grows and moves out into the world.

As you read the thumbnail sketches that follow, first, consider each to be broadly suggestive of circumstances and behaviors, fitting the essential pattern but not necessarily the unique reality of every particular parent/child pair. Second, remember what the child contributes to the interaction; the mother and father of the avoidant or ambivalent child may not be unwilling or unloving parents, but ones who are perhaps simply inaccurately and unhelpfully responsive to their youngster's innate temperament.

Psychologists and other social scientists who study human development have put forth various theories of infant personality, most focusing on qualities of temperament, or the biological tendency to respond to the world in particular ways. One such theory describes temperament as being revealed in three aspects—emotionality, activity, and sociability. The highly emotional youngster reacts quickly and strongly to what's going on around him, displaying extreme delight or extreme unhappiness, for example, in situations that might leave another child unmoved. Activity, in these researchers' definitions, refers to how lively a child tends to be, on a continuum from highly active and squirmy to quiet and languid. Finally, some children are temperamentally inclined to be sociable—they find people interesting and want to be with them—while others are more private and aloof.

Other researchers—notably, Alexander Thomas, Stella Chess, and their colleagues in the New York Longitudinal Study—suggest that most youngsters are temperamentally either easy, difficult, or slow to warm up. The easy child takes most matters in stride. She's pretty content most of the time, and not unduly bothered by novelty or temporary discomforts. This is the baby who quickly settles into feeding and sleeping patterns. The difficult child kicks up a storm over changes in routine or anything new and different. She's easily frustrated, often crying, and irregular in her feeding and sleeping habits. And the slow-to-warm-up child is somewhere in between. She adjusts and adapts, but it takes her a while to get there.

Temperament, many researchers believe, may have a strong genetic basis; babies may come into the world with a nervous system wired to respond to stimuli in these various ways. But that wiring constitutes only a predisposition, not a fate. What's more important to how a child develops, according to Thomas and Chess and other researchers, is "goodness of fit," or how that child's temperament meshes with the world she finds herself in—in particular, how empathetically and helpfully her mother responds to it.

Goodness of fit explains how a cranky, irritable, difficult, standoffish, or in other ways not "easy" baby might develop a more comfortable, accepting and relaxed adjustment to life. That adjustment comes about when her parent or parents give her what she needs—patience, perhaps, or more soothing pats and strokes, or more stimulation, or more quiet—to begin to regulate her own emotions.

The three sketches you're about to read are heavily weighted toward the parent's contribution to attachment development, or, we might say, toward the nurture part of the nature-versus-nurture outcome. Based on the results of several long-term studies, most attachment theorists agree that while a child's temperament is unarguably a critical part of the mix, a parent's behavior toward her child—how sensitively she responds to all those temperamental signals—is infinitely more significant.

THE SECURE CHILD

Jenny's caregivers are appropriately cued in to her needs and attuned to her rhythms. Whatever the details of their caretaking, they respond reliably, consistently, and in a timely manner. Although it may not be an especially easy negotiation between baby and caregiver, they manage to accomplish it well enough.

Jenny doesn't always get her own way, but when she does attempt to make contact, Mom acts thoughtfully. When Jenny cries at night, Mom comes in to pick her up or to stroke her back—possibly after giving her some time to calm herself. When she's feeling anxious and needs some cuddling, Mom cuddles. When she's contentedly amusing herself by reaching for her toes or gazing at the wallpaper with interest, Mom leaves her alone. When she initiates a little babbling, Mom answers. Through her parents, Jenny is acquiring a view of the world as an open, flexible, and accessible place over which she has some say.

As she grows, Jenny is weaned from parental protection gradually, and allowed to explore at her own pace. When she doesn't need help, she can pursue appropriate activities on her own. When she needs further information, Mom provides it in a way that's meaningful to her and for the purpose of deepening her understanding and thus her ability to act independently. She likes to share what she's learned with her parents, knowing they'll reinforce, correct, or enhance her observations.

From her parents' ability to set limits, maintain boundaries, and say "no" when a "no" is called for, she learns other lessons—that at times she must wait for something she wants or adapt to someone else's needs, and that she can gain mastery over her feelings of disappointment or anger. She doesn't like it when her parents go out for an evening or off on a short trip, but she comforts herself with the knowledge that they've made sure she's taken care of and they will return.

When Jenny gets to school, she is accustomed to accepting help and utilizing it well. Her general demeanor is expressive and inquisitive. She'll take on a complex task without becoming quickly frustrated, and she asks for attention from her teacher if needed. Usually, she enjoys school, likes being there, and attempts to comply with classroom rules and follow directions. She's a participant who exudes a can-do attitude.

Over time, Jenny gets along pretty well with her peers. Childhood friendships, filled though they are with sweet yearnings, bitter feuds, and intensity of feeling, run fairly smoothly. Since she trusts others and acts predictably, her friends know what she feels and expects, and also what they can expect from her.

Accustomed to receiving empathetic responses from her

caregivers, Jenny is empathetic herself. She can think of solutions to make better a problem she's having with a friend. She'll feel sad when other children are in distress, and happy when someone else has a good time.

As she grows into adolescence, Jenny's relationships continue to be characterized by openness and trust, although she's not necessarily in the "popular" crowd. She enjoys exchanging confidences and listening to friends; she is willing to hear out the other person but will stand up for her own beliefs.

THE AVOIDANT CHILD

Johnny experiences his caregivers as not especially nurturing.

Perhaps Mom or Dad or both are not given to a lot of hugging, cuddling, and kissing, or perhaps he takes slight pleasure in their attempts to comfort him in those ways. Emotional contact between Johnny and his parent is low-key to non-existent. When he fusses and cries, he gets little response, or a reaction that he finds dismissive, rejecting, or insufficient. When he's feeling especially good and happy, no one pays much attention to that mood either. Positive and negative emotions are disavowed, and any display of his more unpleasant feelings—fearfulness, for example—may be met with anger or annoyance. His parents see emotional shakiness as a sign of weakness.

Not achieving what he wants and needs, Johnny learns that he does best and feels most comfortable with his caregivers by acting as if nothing matters and by not complaining. If they come and go without telling him where they'll be and when they'll be back, he accepts their absence with apparent nonchalance. Neither he nor his parent will own up to missing the other after their separation.

Becoming accustomed to feelings of abandonment, Johnny is determined to fend for himself. He won't go to Mom for help or encouragement, because expressions of neediness have always been rebuffed. He won't seek comforting over a scrape or bruise, because his hurt will be dismissed. Often, his parents are critical and restrictive, not wishing to have their opinions or authority questioned.

In school, Johnny often gets good grades, because he's able to concentrate on "just the facts"—screening out emotions makes it easier to focus on intellectual work. To avoid disappointment and protect himself from painful feelings, he'll tend to deny disagreements or any expression of his needs, which are probably not all that clear to him in any case. Since he is averse to conflict, and makes an effort to please another person in order not to attract anger, he often starts to develop an early reputation as a nice, agreeable guy. Conversely, he may come across to peers and teachers as arrogant, overly confident, precociously independent, or even aggressive. He may send the message: "You don't exist for me, and I'm going to be mean to you to prove it."

With a poor model for closeness and intimacy, he fails to extend himself to enter or remain in social relationships. Johnny's friendships often devolve from commonly held interests—a love of baseball or playing the guitar. When the focus is on activity, he feels comfortable.

THE AMBIVALENT CHILD

Julie is never quite sure what reaction she will get when she signals her parent for attention. Mom and Dad may be available, warm, and cuddly; another time, in response to the same signal and under similar circumstances, they'll be unavailable, cold, and rejecting. If Julie cries at night, sometimes she's picked up, sometimes left to scream herself to sleep. Sometimes she's fed more than she wants, sometimes less. Her caregiver often has difficulty allowing her signals to govern what happens next.

Shifting without warning from being close to being distant, Julie's parents are inconsistent also in what makes them angry or pleased about their child, in what they expect or not on a regular basis. They'll impose a limit and then alternately enforce and ignore it. Julie gets effusive praise from Mom for an "A" in spelling; two days later another "A" brings no response. She is often punished for peculiar reasons. When she falls down and bangs up her knee, her father says, "You're not supposed to be playing on the steps; now you have to stay in," while punching her brother and making him cry brings no rebuke. Her mother may ask lots of questions about a problem she's having with a friend, but fail to remind her of a school deadline or medical appointment.

Finding life unpredictable, Julie becomes preoccupied with her parents' moods and constantly tries to figure out what they're thinking and feeling. She tolerates separations badly. Adjusting to school may be a long and torturous process, involving a lot of clinginess. Leaving for a sleepover date is both excessively exciting and excessively anxiety-producing. Once her emotions are stirred up, Julie will not be consoled and soothed, even when the separation ends. The emotional display is intense, but doesn't work to fulfill her needs—to be close to her parent, or, later, to achieve satisfaction from friendships.

She'll make friends with other children, then impulsively break up over trivial issues. Perpetually frustrated in her earliest efforts to influence others with any consistency, she develops unrealistic expectations and attempts to have friends

do what she wants. Although she tests a relationship by demanding availability, she doesn't really expect it—then she
proves herself correct and feels betrayed. Her peers, understandably, are put off by this hard-to-cope-with behavior,
and often find Julie annoying.

Being unable to predict and influence events fosters in ambivalent Julie feelings of insecurity and a lack of self-worth.

PART II

Find Your Attachment Style

In the following chapters we explore in detail the three basic attachment styles—secure, avoidant, and ambivalent—as they are seen in adults. For each, we sketch a profile that shows how these individuals are likely to reveal their dominant attachment pattern in their relationships.

However, as you read, bear in mind that these individuals, exactly as described, do not exist! We are painting our profiles with the thickest of brushes, the broadest of strokes, and the purest of colors. To use another metaphor, the secure, avoidant, or ambivalent individuals that you're about to meet are the one-hundred-proof variety, undiluted by all the myriad traits of personality, life circumstances, learning experiences, and other factors that combine to produce a fully three-dimensional, walking, talking grown-up.

We have, each one of us, a bit of all three in our repertoires. We're apt to display a sprinkling of behaviors from across the styles, depending on a mood we're in, on an impression we wish to make, or on a change we're trying to effect—maybe even on a spicy lunch that left us with a bad attack of heartburn. But we are also, each of us, possessed of a primary attachment style, which will inevitably surface in a relationship with a love partner and especially when that relationship is under stress.

Before we reveal the three profiles, however, we invite you to find your dominant attachment style through the questionnaire presented in the following chapter.

CHAPTER 3

Your Intimacy Profile

THINK of your romantic relationship (or relationships)—the one you may be in currently, the ones you've enjoyed (or rued) in the past. Reflect on your behaviors as one half of a love couple, and then put a check next to each statement in Part A that most *typically* describes your thoughts, feelings, and experiences. (When you're finished, go back to the beginning and consider how your partner might respond. Even better, persuade your partner to come up with his or her conclusions too.) In Part B, you will consider a series of scenarios and respond according to how you might typically react or handle the situation described. Follow the guidelines at the end of the profile to determine your dominant attachment style.

Part A

TRUE   FALSE

☐   ☐   1. I love the beginning of relationships best, the thrill of the chase. Later, I find that the romance gets a little boring.

☐   ☐   2. I don't know how conscious it is, but I think I'm always looking for someone just the opposite of my father/mother.

☐   ☐   3. The thought that my current partner used to be romantically involved with someone else makes me absolutely crazy. On the one hand, I ask for the gory details, but then I don't want to hear about it.

☐   ☐   4. My romances are rocky.

☐   ☐   5. When I've started a romance, I can't wait to introduce my new partner to everyone I know.

☐   ☐   6. My relationships have been full of surprises.

☐   ☐   7. My romantic partners always want to know more about my personal history—my parents, my childhood, and so on—than I feel like telling.

☐   ☐   8. When friends fix me up with someone new, I'm always tempted to cancel.

TRUE　**FALSE**

☐　☐　9. Generally, I don't put a lot of store in the idea that I'm going to meet "the great love of my life."

☐　☐　10. I find going out with a bunch of couples easier on the nerves than one-on-one dates.

☐　☐　11. I'm not big on romantic sorts of gifts.

☐　☐　12. My relationships have been few and far between.

☐　☐　13. Falling in love happens when you meet the right person.

☐　☐　14. At the outset of a relationship, I enjoy the whole process of figuring out somebody new and different.

☐　☐　15. I like it if my old friends like my new boyfriend/girlfriend, but it doesn't bother me much if they don't.

☐　☐　16. I can tell when a romance I'm in is ready to move to a little higher level of involvement.

☐　☐　17. I've had a couple of bad relationships, but I chalk them up to learning experiences—and that they were!

☐　☐　18. My romantic partners feel like my best friends.

TRUE FALSE

☐ ☐ 19. If great sex isn't there at the start of a relationship, it's never going to happen.

☐ ☐ 20. I really want to make love after my partner and I have had a fight, because I feel incredibly sexy right then.

☐ ☐ 21. Variety is the spice of sexual life—new positions, new places, new times of day, new lingerie!

☐ ☐ 22. My partner wants to make love more often than I do, and he/she is the one who usually gets things going.

☐ ☐ 23. Sex is not terribly high on the list of what's important in a relationship.

☐ ☐ 24. It irritates me when my partner wants a lot of cuddling and saying "I love you."

☐ ☐ 25. The best sex is what you get to after a long time with someone you know well.

☐ ☐ 26. When my partner and I have just had a blow-out fight, the last thing I feel like is making love.

☐ ☐ 27. I don't mind hearing a little about my partner's former lovers—but I don't need chapter and verse!

Part B

28. When I have an on-the-job problem to deal with, I

    a. get my partner's advice about what to do, but more often than not I don't follow it.

    b. take care of it on my own.

    c. find my partner sometimes has some helpful input to make.

29. When I'm feeling really sick, I usually like to

    a. be the focus of my partner's undivided attention.

    b. shut the door, pull down the shades, and crawl into bed.

    c. get fussed over a little bit by my partner.

30. When my partner is feeling really sick, I usually

    a. feel upset.

    b. feel annoyed, because he/she always makes a mountain out of a molehill.

    c. suggest he/she call the doctor.

31. When my partner has to go out of town on business, I

    a. feel antsy and unsettled until he/she returns, and even then I still feel sort of depressed for a while.

    b. kind of like being on my own.

    c. miss my partner, but I might use the time to get together with friends with whom I know my partner doesn't especially enjoy socializing.

32. I discover an old bill for flowers (not for me) in my partner's desk drawer. I

   a. immediately accuse my partner of having an affair.

   b. assume the flowers were sent to meet a business obligation, and don't mention it.

   c. worry that my partner is having an affair, and decide I'll have to ask him/her outright.

33. My partner cheated on me some years back. Although we reconciled, I

   a. can't help bringing it up when something goes wrong between us.

   b. felt cooler from then on toward my partner, but I see no point in talking about the affair any more.

   c. know real damage was done to our relationship, but I am confident that the damage will heal over time.

34. When my partner objects to the time I spend away from him/her with my family or pursuing some private hobbies and interests, I

   a. challenge him/her, because I don't think he/she has any right to object.

   b. agree to cut back, but then I usually don't.

   c. try to oblige.

35. If my partner hung a picture in our house that I really can't stand, without consulting me, I would

   a. take it down.

   b. ignore it.

c. tell my partner I can't stand that picture.

36. When we have some vacation days to spend, I like to
   a. take off in the car and see where we end up.
   b. leave the arrangements up to my partner.
   c. make careful plans.

37. When we're faced with a major crisis, I tend to
   a. have a hard time settling on a course of action.
   b. take action for my partner and myself.
   c. research the problem exhaustively.

38. If my partner bought himself/herself a pricey leather jacket, even though we've agreed to stick to a tight budget, I would
   a. buy something for myself.
   b. ask whether he/she has taken on a second job unbeknownst to me (and also resolve privately to start a separate account of my own).
   c. read him/her the riot act, then simmer down and bring up the budget thing again.

39. When my partner and I have a big disagreement, I tend to
   a. keep at it until he/she sees things my way.
   b. tune out.
   c. let the whole thing drop, because life is too short to keep on arguing.

40. When my partner gets his/her way on an issue that's really important to me, I

a. don't talk to him/her afterward.

b. figure I'll let him/her have this one and I'll take the next one.

c. don't mind compromising.

41. When, after a big fight, my partner says, "Let's make up, don't go to bed mad," I generally respond,

a. "Maybe I'm not ready to make up, just because you are."

b. "There's nothing to make up about."

c. "Sure, give me a kiss, but this isn't over yet."

42. My partner doesn't want sex very often and is difficult to arouse. I

a. think he/she doesn't love me.

b. have sex occasionally and let it go.

c. bring up the painful and embarrassing subject of what might make sex more pleasurable.

43. My partner wants sex more often than I do. I

a. think that he/she might be oversexed.

b. explain that I have a low sex drive.

c. try to be more accommodating.

44. When my partner asks me what it was like for me growing up, I

a. enjoy telling him/her about that nightmare scene.

b. don't have a lot to say. My parents were fine.

c. realize I can see those two titans of my youth with some degree of objectivity.

45. When we're at a big party where neither of us knows many people, I

   a. insist we leave.

   b. point out I didn't want to go in the first place.

   c. will stick around longer than I want to if my partner seems to be having some fun.

The responses to these statements involve the degree of intimacy within a relationship, or classic attachment style issues—trust, privacy, dependency, conflict, anxiety, and separation.

If you've answered true for numbers 1 through 6 and 19 through 21, and come up with mostly "a" answers for numbers 28 through 45, your intimacy profile reveals an essentially *ambivalent* style.

If you've answered true for numbers 7 through 12 and 22 through 24 and you have mostly "b" answers for 28 through 45, you display an *avoidant* style.

A *secure* style is suggested by true responses for 13 through 18 and 25 through 27 and a preponderance of "c" answers for 28 through 45.

In the next three chapters, we'll look a little more closely at just what that all means.

But first, this thought: It will probably have been apparent to you that the "secure" responses suggest a mostly reasonable and balanced approach to life. The individual who came up secure is one who, when handling conflict, dealing with separations, accepting people, and so on, seems to have his or her head screwed on right. And as we'll see in the chapters to come, although the secure is far from perfect and hardly immune to relationship troubles, by and large he or she does present an appealing persona—confident, caring, clear-headed, and empathetic.

Which is how we all wish to be! If you have rated yourself squarely in the secure category, you may indeed have a secure attachment style. On the other hand, a majority of secure responses to the preceding 45 statements may reflect your understandable human desire to see yourself in the best light. You may also unconsciously want to persuade yourself that you possess qualities that clearly will be useful in maintaining or promoting the love relationship you're in.

Later in this book, you will hear the conversations of several couples who participated in a survey we conducted on attachment styles and couple fits. The dialogues we present were culled from several dozen couples, all of whom first individually filled out questionnaires similar to the profile you have just completed. From their responses on paper, we rated the majority of those individuals as secure. From their videotaped interactions with each other, however, we determined that many of these self-described secures were either avoidant or ambivalent.

The point is, we all have difficulty seeing ourselves objectively. You may have tended to come up with "pleasing" answers, while overlooking or downplaying aspects of your relationship behaviors that seem more anxiety ridden or simply less flattering. For a better couple fit, you will find it most useful to work at understanding and accepting all three styles, and at rigorously examining your own tendencies with a cool eye. Here's one more suggestion we would make: After you have finished reading the following chapters, and had an inside look at how attachment styles are revealed in the day-to-day struggles of the couples you will meet there, come back and take our intimacy profile again. From that more informed perspective, see whether your self-assessment takes on a different shape.

CHAPTER 4

The Secure

SHE may be a gregarious leader, the student government president who went on to become a high-voltage attorney or businessperson. Or she may be contemplative and quiet, the kid who always marched to her own drummer and who finds adult contentment from a loyal group of friends and a low-key job.

Whatever the contours of her temperament or circumstances, she meets life pretty squarely. She is secure.

The Secure Is:

• **responsive to feelings, the positive and negative, his own and the other guy's.** He can give a hug of affection and say "I love you" without feeling exposed and vulnerable.

He can express dissatisfaction with another's words or actions without destroying the friendship.

He can respond empathetically to another's sadness or anxiety without being overwhelmed by those emotions himself.

He can honor a partner's need for solitude or silence without feeling threatened.

• **not fearful of confrontation.** In the summer after her junior year in college, Nikki worked as an intern in a record company. One day when her co-worker was talking on the phone to their boss about some bit of business, Nikki heard her name mentioned. After the call, Nikki asked her colleague whether Jake, the boss, had said something about her; the colleague told her that Jake had asked him whether he thought Nikki was "into guys or girls."

Nikki talked over the incident with her mother and with several friends, and then, with some trepidation, indicated to Jake that she'd like to speak to him. In that conversation, she told her boss that she would like him not to discuss her with co-workers, and that if he had questions about her personal life he should ask her and she would then decide if she wished to answer them.

Here's Nikki sometime later, one year into her marriage with Joe, a fellow who's often determined to do what he wants. As they are about to throw their first big party, Joe decides that afternoon to join a couple of buddies to play basketball, promising to be home in plenty of time to pick up the ice and help her set things out. Nikki isn't happy, but can't persuade him to skip the basketball. Later, Joe blows in the front door when half their guests have already arrived, says his hellos, then dashes in to take a quick shower.

Nikki excuses herself from her company, follows Joe to the bedroom, and shuts the door. She says, "You have just treated me badly. Now, I'm going to have a good time tonight and see that our friends have a good time, and then you and I are going to talk." That night, they do. Nikki is mad as hell—rightly, Joe concedes—and he's apologetic to a fault. She stays angry for a couple of days, and then, once over it, explains to her husband again how his behavior upset her evening, made more work for her, added to her nervousness about hosting a big party for the first time, and hurt her feelings.

In these two stories, we can trace hallmarks of secure behavior: Confrontation may not be pleasant, or easy, but the secure takes it on anyway when she believes it's the proper course. She speaks her piece clearly, perhaps after reasoning out her thoughts on the matter. She doesn't launch a personal attack on the other guy, but conveys to him her feelings, sticking to the issue. She won't bury those feelings of anger at the first sign of apology if she senses he's still unable or unwilling to appreciate why she reacted the way she did.

• **eager to let bygones be bygones.** Because she is responsive to other people, and because she's happier being glad than staying mad, it's not hard for the secure to forgive and forget and move on. Letting bygones be bygones works to restore and strengthen the couple fit.

When Nikki, for example, got over being angry, she was over it. Having gained some insight, the hard way, into her partner's tendency to get carried away with what he likes to do and to play time to its limits, she almost surely will be more on her guard the next party night and insist on a greater degree of pulling together. What she *won't* do, however, is hold this one endlessly against Joe, and resurrect it as a still active grievance when he forgets to pick up the cat food on his way home or doesn't refill the ice cube trays.

• **overly accommodating.** That talent at making up and moving on, and the wish to get back to life on a pleasant note, can lead the secure to underplay issues that need more thrashing out. Especially in a relationship with an avoidant or an ambivalent, a secure might think, "I really want some changes here but hey, I love the guy, I can live with what I'm getting, so I'll let the matter drop." She *can* live with it, but possibly at the cost of stifling a full range of emotional expression.

• **willing to see two sides to a story.** Hearing another's point of view, becoming frustrated, and negotiating the tough stuff are challenges the secure can tolerate.

Max and Jerry, two young men who graduated from business school together, are starting a company offering a highly specialized kind of computer retraining. Max describes himself as "the money man and the organizer." (He's the money man because the financing for their venture came from his father.) He calls Jerry "the carny barker," since he's out drumming up business and hatching ideas for a range of as yet undesigned and possibly unmarketable products. Before too long, it becomes clear to Max that he and Jerry are on different wavelengths, and Max is getting edgy about a number of issues—for example, establishing a responsible repayment plan with his father and figuring out a more sensible allotment of profits. For his part, Jerry appears not to see any problem, and is rarely on the premises long enough to pick up on his friend's concerns.

Recognizing a need to act on his increasing discomfort, Max tells Jerry they're going to remove themselves for "a two-man think-tank session," away from the office and with plenty of time. After the fact, Max described it as "a real come-to-Jesus meeting," in which he voiced his worries, gained a truer understanding of Jerry's vision, and then made them stay up all night writing out a long-range business plan that satisfied them both.

Although he does have an emotional reaction to what he perceives as his friend's recklessness, Max displays secure behavior, having little trouble sticking to content and maintaining a thoughtful, analytic approach to a real problem with more than one side to consider. He can see the world from Jerry's point of view, still be aware of his own interests, and direct their talk steadily toward a solution.

• **able to discover options.** The secure knows that she can influence her life. In a crisis or at a fork in the road, she will think things out and consider options. And she'll seek out and accept the advice and good counsel of others in finding those alternative paths and solutions.

Consider Diane, for example, married to Jim for twenty years. Five years into that marriage, Jim had an affair that almost wrecked them. Actions she took in the wake of that chaos helped her stick with and ultimately find contentment in a less than ideal union.

"I had two babies, no career," she says. "I felt furious and betrayed. I knew I had to make some decisions fast, and I found a wonderful therapist who helped me sort things through. What I realized was that I wanted to stay with Jimmy, who—despite everything else—was a lot of fun, a loving father, and sexually attractive to me." He still is, she says, and those pluses swayed the balance. Once she had it straight in her own mind about what she wanted, and what she reasonably could expect from her partner, she entered graduate school as soon as her youngest child started kindergarten, got a master's in social work, and began a career that, she says, "many times over the years has been my safe haven."

Like Diane, the secure can realistically modify her expectations, explore options, and find more than one way to attain a sense of personal satisfaction.

• **in danger of missing the fun in life.** Especially when a secure is burdened with perhaps more than his fair share of problems, his sense of "doing what's right" can squeeze a lot of the pleasure out of life. But even when things are going smoothly, the secure's responsible approach can make him resistant to letting loose. A secure might be a rather dry fellow.

• **trusting.** In a romantic relationship, the secure will accept his partner's need to take a particular action, even if it is one he'd rather she didn't or one he doesn't quite understand.

Eliot demonstrates this capacity in his reaction to his fiancée Ann's declaration that she wants to spend a long summer with her family, two thousand miles away. Ann, who has just resigned from her position in an investment banking house, will be starting graduate school in the fall, and has four months off. She is mentally readying herself for a new career and eventual marriage to Eliot. Contemplating the longest stretch of free time she's ever had, and somewhat concerned also about aging parents and an estranged sister, Ann feels the time is ripe to "go home again," enjoy her parents and reassure them of her well-being, and mend some fences.

The idea makes Eliot unhappy—he will miss her terribly; he also has reservations about her belief that getting together with her family now will leave Ann feeling better. But he trusts her judgment that she needs to make this visit. He tells her: "Well, this is going to be the longest three months of my life, without you here. I'd rather you didn't go. But you're the one who knows what you need to do for yourself and your family, and I don't. So we'll have some gargantuan phone bills for a while."

Able to tune in to the other's feelings, the secure will take it on faith that the partner is acting in his or her best interests. That's an ability, as we will see, that makes a separation a far less angst-ridden affair than it is for the ambivalent or the avoidant, for each of whom separating from a partner stirs deepest fears of personal rejection and abandonment.

• **complacent.** Gina describes herself as the one member of her family "whose head is screwed on straight." She regularly runs interference among her scatty, nervous mother, her overbearing older brother Bob, and her younger sister Gwen, who has suffered serious bouts of depression. Lately, largely through Gina's efforts, life is running smoothly—Bob has come to accept their mother's difficult nature, Gwen is getting the professional help she needs, and everyone is on good speaking terms. When the three siblings met for dinner and a letting-their-hair-down talk one evening, Gina heard some assessments of herself that brought her up short. "Gina is the girl with all the answers," said Gwen, not unaffectionately. "Do you know," Bob said to Gina, with a smile, "how goddamn irritating you can be?"

Confident in herself, sure of what she knows and can accomplish, the secure may come across as a tad smug.

• **naive.** While at a party, twenty-three-year-old Lexie met a man whom she liked on sight. He apparently felt the same attraction, and called her, she says, "at least twice a day for the next three or four weeks. We went out every other night. Very intense. He was even telling me he couldn't wait for his mother to meet me. Then, abruptly, nothing. I didn't hear from him." She was devastated. Anticipating an enjoyable and long-term romance with a man she had chosen, Lexie couldn't make sense of his sudden rejection.

Like most secures, Lexie likes people and tends to think the best of them. She lacks that touch of suspiciousness that might have kept her from making a bad judgment. And also like most secures, she's used to being on an even keel and having things go her way. When they don't, she's thrown for a loop. The secure can be a bit naive, with a "problems aren't supposed to happen to me" outlook.

• **smart about her own dumb moves.** She can pull herself up by the bootstraps, though, get a grip on her dismay, and rein in negative behaviors before they go too far.

For example, Lexie resisted the urge to phone her boyfriend, took "a lot of very long walks to think," and ran her thoughts by her best friend. "That kind of more-than-all or less-than-nothing behavior—plus the fact that I found out he lied to me about the kind of work he did—is not a good sign," she concluded. "This guy was not one for the long haul."

Seeing the negative possibilities that might have developed if she had proceeded, and being neither impulsive nor in denial of apparent realities, Lexie stopped herself from acting against her own best interest.

The secure is not necessarily a goody-goody. She may drink too much, dabble in drugs, or flirt with over-the-top behaviors of one sort or another. But at some point, a small, internal, limiting voice tells her: "Back off. You're going too far. Quit this. This may be truly dangerous." And then, if necessary, she will find good help.

• **tolerant of differences.** The secure accepts and even welcomes differences in his partners.

Here's Willem, speaking about his lover, Natalia: "You know, I'm typically Swiss. Everything you Americans say about us is true—it's no accident that the Swiss are known for making excellent watches. But what I like about my Italian girlfriend is that she's so different. For me, that's the fun of it. She's more casual, for one thing—which means we never get anywhere on time! That's just the way she's made."

• **a friend in deed and in need.** Being tolerant of differences makes the secure a sturdy friend. Secures are not especially jealous or possessive; they allow their friends independence and enjoy ever widening and enriching the circle by introducing one to the other.

And when life goes sour on a friend, the secure is on the scene.

Penny's close friend Samantha suffered a shattering blow when her fiancé broke their engagement one month before an elaborately planned wedding. Her friends, Penny among them, rallied around to be consoling and to help deal with the messy business of canceling all the arrangements. Some months after Sam was dumped, although most of her crowd had grown impatient with Sam's emotional fragility, Penny keenly sensed and accepted her friend's continuing neediness. She let it be known that she was on call, at three A.M. if necessary, if Sam wanted to talk. She came by Sam's office after work on a regular basis, knowing her friend was tending to race back to her apartment every evening to stare at TV all night, and took her out for a beer and a burger. Slowly, as Sam showed signs of healing, Penny dragged her out to some social events and casual parties. Much later, Samantha talks about getting through that bleak time only with the help of her friend, "a one-woman support team and trauma unit."

• **confident in love.** Secure lovers describe their relationships as mostly happy, friendly, and trusting—although those connections are not necessarily trouble free. They get angry, they have fights, they face crises over which they may start down separate paths. The good part is that secures will attempt to reach agreement, without resentments or the sense on the part of one or the other of "giving in." And then, that ability to let bygones be bygones comes to the fore; the bad feelings are resolved and the original emotional state is remembered and can be recaptured.

In her love relationship, the secure is capable of setting limits, which is a skill critical to both the comfort level and the growth possibilities in any couple fit. She can tell her perhaps not-so-securely-attached partner, "This is my territory, that's yours," or "This is what I'd like more of from you, and this is what I would like less of." She may not *get* what she hopes for; she may let her overly accommodating tendency come to the fore. But she's able to define and articulate her boundaries.

Secure married relationships tend to last, with few divorces. That said, when a secure makes up her mind that a marriage is intolerable, which is usually when there has been an ongoing breach of trust, she'll end it, without long drawn-out battles or a lot of agonizing and second-guessing. And, after a period of healing, she's willing to trust again, viewing life as an ongoing proposition.

Does the secure seem to suggest a vision of impossible, perpetual sunniness? As we'll see in the chapters ahead, he's not always a sunny fellow at all, and, indeed, not always living in a bed of roses. He may realize his dreams or experience more than his fair share of regrets and disappointments, and may even fall for an impossibly difficult partner. His great strength, however, comes from an ability to derive deep enjoyment from the good that life has to offer; his second great strength lies in his willingness to put in the effort to bring his partner along with him.

CHAPTER 5

The Avoidant

HE may be the cool, stoic cowboy type like Gary Cooper in *High Noon*—calm, controlled, and, at all times, seemingly in charge.

He may be ambitious, a nonconformist, a workaholic.

Whatever his life's path, confronting emotions, the good and the bad, is difficult to impossible. He's avoidant.

The Avoidant Is:

• **distant.** "I don't even shake hands," says Jack, a college professor. "I wave to people instead." Jack, a sweet and witty guy, is undoubtedly poking a little fun at himself, but his jest carries a kernel of truth. The fact is, Jack—like some avoidants—is most content on his own. He keeps social contacts to the minimum, and to spare himself the difficulties of meeting women in conventional settings, advertises in personal columns.

• **a dodger of conflict.** Consider Holden Caufield, the appealingly romantic hero of J. D. Salinger's *Catcher in the Rye*, and you might see beneath the recognizably unhappy teenager the shape of an avoidant, always heading away from unpleasantness. Holden runs off from school following a conflict with a teacher; from the hotel after a conflict with a clerk; even, finally, from his beloved sister Phoebe, walking away from her in the rain. Seeing the conditional nature of reality as too much to face, he refuses the work of getting to know people and prefers snap judgments instead, labeling most others "phonies" at once.

Like Holden, avoidants generally are most comfortable with absolutes, which relieve them of the necessity of sorting through a myriad of both negative and positive emotions, and which seem to simplify life.

• **oblivious to moods and feelings, both his own and those of others.** The avoidant prefers an intellectual process, devoid of emotional response. Because his goal in a relationship is to maintain distance, he tries not to respond to situations with emotional overtones. Moods and feelings are just too messy. Besides, expressing feelings may lead to conflict, and conflict will lead to abandonment.

In social situations, he'll tend to give "lectures," as opposed to engaging in the rich ebb and flow of a mutual sharing of opinion.

• **good in a crisis.** Because he *does* feel most comfortable approaching matters intellectually, the avoidant is good in a crisis or at times of family stress. He's able to set feelings aside (more likely, deny them entirely) and take charge at some of life's thornier moments. He's not overwhelmed by new situations.

• **someone who likes peace at any price (sort of).** Contrary to her public image, the avoidant isn't all that genuinely agreeable. Disliking any display of feelings, she is contained, while silently, internally, she's keeping score. She will suppress her disagreement or discontent, say nothing, then suddenly, out of nowhere, blow up. Her refusal to discuss differences, and her then possible subsequent eruption, make life difficult, and certainly confusing, for her friends or partner.

Here's one of those out-of-the-blue mini-explosions from Sean, who lives with his girlfriend, Alicia. Alicia has been helping out her younger sister, Emily, who has just graduated from college and moved into a small apartment. Emily is often invited to join Alicia and Sean for spaghetti dinners, which Sean apparently enjoys. Alicia also gives Emily some of her old clothing and, on occasion, five or ten bucks. One evening, as Emily leaves, Alicia hands her a one-pound can of coffee from their larder, because Emily had mentioned she's out at home. As soon as the door closes, Sean explodes, shouting at his girlfriend that coffee is damned expensive; he's limiting himself to one cup at night, and here she is giving it away.

If we could see a list of those scores Sean has been racking up, it might say that Alicia gave her sister a box of cereal last week, or Emily is around too much, or Alicia was rude to his brother last month. It *wouldn't* say they can't afford a can of coffee. But the avoidant is suddenly reminded of a bunch of other "wrongs," grievances he has been holding but of which he's said nothing.

Here is another aspect to the peace-at-any-price drive: In the avoidant's extreme need to keep the heat off and not stir things up, in his reluctance to ask for what he wants or express a differing opinion (because then he'll be attacked or abandoned), he will pass the dirty business on to somebody else.

For example, Marcy suggests that she and her fiancé, Fred, take a part share in a ski lodge condo one winter. Fred hates the idea; he thinks the place is too expensive, too crowded, and too far away to visit often, but in his avoidant way, says merely, "Well, maybe, we'll think about it." When time is running out and Marcy presses for an answer from Fred, he invites his sister to join them for drinks one evening, knowing this sister had a thoroughly miserable experience in just such a skiing arrangement. The sister pooh-poohs the condo plan, points out ten things that could go wrong, and ends up in a minor spat with Marcy, accusing her of steamrolling Fred.

Avoidant Fred has shifted the confrontation to another party, while he remains in his seemingly neutral corner.

• **unspontaneous.** He likes what he likes and sees no reason to change or experiment. He'll eat the same meal in the same restaurant every day (and never will attempt ethnic cuisine). Careful and methodical planning for the future gives him the greatest sense of satisfaction, comfort, and control.

That lack of spontaneity can make the avoidant a difficult lover, for one thing. Even when he wants to make his partner happy, he is often too rigid and withholding to be receptive to requests for new ways of lovemaking or more holding and cuddling.

• **a stalwart partner.** For the spouse or lover who isn't bothered by that lack of spontaneity, or who doesn't feel a desperate and unhappy need for greater disclosure and intimacy, the avoidant can be a wonderful mate—solid, reliable, responsible. When she has settled on her partner, she's in for the long haul.

• **fearful of dependency.** Possessed of a powerful urge to prove he relies on no one, his perfectly normal dependency needs go unacknowledged and unmet.

The avoidant has always developed strategies for taking care of himself (and has little tolerance for people who can't do the same). He may be the one in the family to shop and prepare dinner or is the family bookkeeper. He won't lean on anyone, and doesn't want them leaning on him either.

Alex and his girlfriend Lindsay made plans to do some in-line skating, but on that afternoon Alex arrives at her apartment looking green around the gills. After her several inquiries into what's bothering him, Alex admits he's under the weather and woke up with aches and pains and a fever. Lindsay immediately suggests they should then stay in and she'll heat up some soup, but Alex insists he's fine, and tells her to get her skates.

Avoidantly, Alex can't accept his friend's pointing up his real need, which is to be comforted and coddled a little. Instead of acknowledging her offer of support—and accepting it—he prefers to state a fact ("I'm sick") and retreat from any feelings on the matter, acting as if they don't exist.

Even when he has *asked* for support, the avoidant may be unable to accept it. For example, Marshall has been working like a dog getting his independent graphic design business off the ground, and he talks at length to his girlfriend Connie about his hunt for new clients. Connie, a freelance editor and proofreader, meets a publisher who is putting together a new magazine and who says he might be able to use Marshall's services. Thrilled, Connie passes this lead on to her boyfriend. Marshall never calls to follow up.

This avoidant man is feeling pushed, suddenly laden with his girlfriend's expectations that he must now meet, and perhaps fearful of possible rejection or failure. Then he shuts down or even resents her efforts, and avoids acting in his own interest.

• **Mr. Nice Guy.** Because he dislikes conflict and disagreement, an avoidant often seems like an extremely nice guy to friends and acquaintances: agreeable, easy to please, and eager to please others. When friends switch plans or arrive late, he won't get ruffled. He may like to live modestly and dress simply; it's part of his nice guy self-image. He likes, too, to be kind to strangers and underdogs, a form of giving that requires of him only a superficial level of emotional connection.

"People have stopped me on the street to tell me what a great guy I'm married to," says Jane, referring to Tom, her husband of ten years, whom, in fact, she is about to leave. Tom spends many hours volunteering at a free meals program in a local church, and invites the people he helps there to call him if they're feeling lonely or need to talk. And they do. Unfortunately, he finds it impossible to talk to his wife, other than to pass along an amusing anecdote or inquire about plans for the day, and she is frustrated, pained, and dismayed.

An avoidant can become overly concerned about doing what's best for an outsider, while failing to behave in a realistically protective manner toward himself or his loved one. He may interpret dependency in a partner as a sign of weakness, and weakness is intolerable, in himself or someone close to him.

Helen asks her husband, Warren, to accompany her to her office one evening—she is uneasy about the security. Warren's response is to mock her for being such a "nervous Nellie." A few days earlier, however, Warren had mentioned to Helen that he'd walked one of his co-workers to her car because it was late in the evening and he was concerned for her safety. Like many avoidants, this man has learned to act in a socially acceptable fashion. He has no trouble seeing that it's appropriate to provide security to a young woman who has worked late at his request, but with someone of central emotional importance, such as Helen, Warren reverts to his avoidant style.

The avoidant's nice guy persona can be confusing to his partner in the early stages of a love relationship. She's likely to see this potential boyfriend as charming, independent, and positive, just the way so many others see him. He can even *sound* nicely intimate. If she listens closely, however, she may detect the persistent determination to swim well above emotional waters.

• **often a great success in his chosen career.** In the chapters to come, you'll meet what we call the well-socialized avoidant, an individual who is a hit in the world at large. This is someone who has good manners, good conversation, poise, and intelligence—plus, the ability to tune out messy human distractions and focus on getting the job done. In addition, the workplace may be an avoidant's refuge and comfort, an arena in which her cool competence is usually admired and rewarded.

• **in need of lots of praise.** Dorothea and her two pals, Tessa and Devon, have planned to take in a concert at Tanglewood, three hundred miles from where they live. Dorothea decides to do all the driving and they reach the concert grounds in under five hours, with a stop midway for lunch. She's pleased with herself—and silently fuming at her friends, who have expressed no appreciation of her driving skills. She says nothing as they arrange their gear on the lawn. Later, at their motel, Tessa remarks, "Hey, Doe, you were a genius behind the wheel today. I never thought we'd make it in time." Dorothea beams, and mentions the miles-per-hour pace she maintained.

Avoidant Dorothea wants a little attention and praise, but won't indicate as much. If her friend hadn't spontaneously given her the pat on the back, she would continue feeling rejected, unrewarded, and probably unloved as well.

Not asking for what they want and need, avoidants hardly ever get it.

• **often passive aggressive and/or sarcastic.** Like everyone, of course, the avoidant does *have* powerful emotions. But because it's uncomfortable to deal with them in an up-front way, she may become sarcastic or express feelings through nonverbal behaviors. If she is anxious or angry, she may be late for an appointment or forget it completely. She'll indicate her annoyance by losing her house keys or forgetting where she put her wallet, causing a problem for her partner and herself.

Here is a classic passive-aggressive bit of acting out: Maureen agreed to pick her husband up at the airport, although she didn't want to. Rather than tell him so, she arrived an hour late. She says: "Frank was furious at having to wait around for me. But he shouldn't have asked me in the first place. My afternoons are always so rushed, I don't have time to be a car service."

In later chapters, we will see some examples of unkindly sarcastic behavior. We call this the avoidant's tendency to use the sword (the bitter word) to kill her love, pushing the partner back to a distance at which she feels more comfortable.

• **unconscious of past hurts.** The avoidant tends to view her parents, for example, as idealized, apple pie figures, with no warts or bumps.

One evening, Diana reminisces about her parents with her best friend, Andrea. Among the stories she tells: She wasn't supposed to cry, even when her father extracted a wiggly baby tooth with his pliers. Her mother taught her to swim by taking her out into the ocean, at a depth over her head, then letting her go and refusing to give her a helping hand, an experience Diana thinks put her off ocean swimming forever after. Her parents would often say on a Saturday or Sunday, "Come on, we're going in the car," and Diana wouldn't know where they were headed until they arrived at Grandma's or at a friend's house.

These sound like rather unhappy tales to Andrea, who also remembers that her friend often speaks proudly of the fact that she's been living on her own and supporting herself since she was eighteen. "Jeez," says Andrea, "I bet you're not in the biggest rush to see your mom and pop again." But Diana has been smiling as she tells those stories, and now she shakes her head and laughs. Oh no, she says, her parents are the most wonderful, strong, independent, interesting, and creative people.

By closing off her need for closeness, comfort, and soothing, Diana is able to remain unhurt by her own childhood. An avoidant, too, is often able to get out of a punitive or chilly home early and quickly, although she cannot say just why she left. Admitting to a stressful home life requires facing feelings.

- **therapy challenged.** Don't expect the avoidant willingly to talk about what is wrong, much less embrace the idea of going for help. His attitude: Don't dwell on your problems and they'll go away; just get over it.

- **slow to love.** Afraid of intimacy, he lacks trust. In fact, he has trouble believing in love—he might say that love is hard to find and question whether it can ever last. When he does cast his lot, though, he's likely to be faithful to his one and only, and happiest if that lover idealizes him as the perfect man.

But casting his lot is a challenge. An avoidant pattern can surface as early as the first date. This is the guy who can't quite fix on the time to meet, or says, "I'll call you later in the week and we'll make a plan."

An avoidant lover, like Jonathan, can also be good at disappearing, then reappearing. Jonathan had been dating Whitney for half a year; they spent weekends together and took a couple of Caribbean vacations together. She considered herself his girlfriend. One morning after they had spent the previous night at her apartment, Jonathan jotted a note to Whitney—"Give me a call after you have that meeting with your boss"—and left it on the kitchen counter before heading off to work. Whitney read the note, and discovered that it was written on the back of a wedding invitation. It was the wedding of one of Jonathan's close friends that had taken place two weeks earlier and apparently Jonathan had attended—unbeknownst to her.

Jonathan, avoidantly, was involving Whitney in only part of his life, and then came up with an avoidant method of letting her find that out. She asked him to explain, then decided the relationship probably had no future and broke it off. A year later, he called, wanting to take her out. A year after that, he called again, suggesting dinner. After a sufficiently comfortable distance was re-established, he had no problem with—and saw nothing amiss in—popping up once more.

When an avoidant is pushed to say what he wants, he'll become angry and blame his partner for being "controlling." Faced with a statement of what his *partner* wants (especially if that involves requests for further intimacy), he'll feel criticized and unloved, and further withdraw. Even a mild, un-threatening suggestion rings in his ears as a reproach. The quality of his attachment behavior may always carry with it that strong scent of anger, which sends the message: "Don't get too close to me."

Once ensconced in a relationship, the avoidant lover is a hoarder of affection. He's not a big hugger or kisser; indeed, he feels he possesses only a fixed quantity of love, an easily depleted supply of hugs and kisses. He has trouble under-standing that the more affection he gives out, the more he gets back. He aims, too, to attain a sense of coolly comfort-able accommodation, and is content to let the passion fade.

Listening to Rick (Humphrey Bogart) explaining the score to Ilsa (Ingrid Bergman) in *Casablanca*—"Where I'm going you can't go. What I'm doing you can't have any part of"—can we hear the voice of the avoidant-in-love? Rick, whom we'll be so bold as to label the archetypical avoidant, won't let their love revive. Instead, he uses patriotism (perhaps the avoidant's last refuge) to resist her strong emotional pull and lofty ideals to defend against involvement.

These are a few of the typical characteristics of the avoid-ant, who sounds like a handful! But with some help from friends and lovers, he or she can learn to become greatly more responsive to the feelings of others and more expressive of his or her own.

CHAPTER 6

The Ambivalent

IF she can't be the life of the party, she's usually found sulking on the sidelines. She may be an artist, a writer, a psychiatrist—rarely, however, a true team player.

Dynamic and creative, perhaps also maddeningly scatty, she rides a perpetual rollercoaster. She wants what she wants, passionately, and pulls it toward her. When she achieves her goal, however, she often pushes it away. She's ambivalent.

The Ambivalent Is:

• **oppositional.** First and foremost, this is one resistant person. An ambivalent feels compelled to oppose a course of action suggested by another, be it as simple as leaving ten minutes earlier than planned to catch a train or using the blue glasses instead of the clear glasses for iced tea. A simple interaction may easily prompt a negotiation or an argument.

Major issues are rarely resolved once and for all, arising repeatedly as brand-new, never-before-considered situations. Prior decisions are revisited and may be easily tossed aside.

In fact, the ambivalent is in opposition to himself a lot of the time and finds that making any significant decision is a painful business, accompanied as it is by immediate thoughts of the alternatives. In an effort to relieve that internal pressure, he cuts to the chase, without a lot of talk or careful deliberation.

• **girded for battle.** The negotiations and arguments can escalate, in the blink of an eye, into fights. This individual, perpetually needing to keep the pot roiling, has one foot over the battle line at any given time. (Our secure, on the other hand, is hanging around the line, ready to go either way, while the avoidant remains way, way behind the line.)

Ambivalent Arthur, his parents, and a small group of friends are having dinner in a noisy, lively Italian restaurant, in which the specialty of the house is *pasta con mare*, served from one giant bowl in the middle of the table. While the other members of the party are emitting satisfied *mmm's* and *ahh's* over this fragrant feast, Arthur looks annoyed. He calls the waiter over to complain about the skimpy amount of lobster in the bowl, saying that they had more last time, and then again to send back a piece of octopus he claims is "solid rubber." On the third summons, he orders a small antipasto for himself alone.

Arthur likes the battle. But part of his tendency to stir things up can be traced to the ambivalent's difficulty in deriving true satisfaction from what's underway at any given time.

When things are going particularly well, in fact, his instinct is to pull back, cutting off experiences that might be gratifying. In later chapters, we'll sometimes refer to this limited ability to "sink into the moment" and to find contentment therein. Always in conflict about where he wants to be or what he should be doing, the ambivalent usually feels vaguely discontented with the activity at hand. Even when he can acknowledge his own good skills or a particular accomplishment, he takes from them little feeling of achievement, or only a temporary one.

• **adventuresome.** Life with an ambivalent is seldom dull. She is often playful, amusing, and full of wonderful ideas and extravagant adventures. She keeps her partner at all times a little off balance, never knowing quite what to expect, which can add a lot of zest to the relationship.

• **bossy and in charge.** The ambivalent expects his needs to be met, although he frequently fails to make them clear. His feelings are constantly shifting; he rarely experiences joy, anger, or pleasure in the absence of the directly opposite emotion. Because of this, the ambivalent has difficulty distinguishing between the positive and the negative going on inside his head. Each conflicting feeling carries equal intensity. *He* doesn't know quite what he wants, so neither do the people around him. At the same time, he wants to feel very much in charge.

For Charles, a trial attorney, this ambivalent characteristic contributed to a critical conflict at work. Charles is a wonderfully effective lawyer; consumed with his cases, he not only handles important commercial matters for his firm but takes on pro bono work as well. Before the firm's executive committee will meet to assign bonuses one year, Henry, the chairman, invites Charles to join him for an after-work drink. In the course of a congenial chat, Henry fulsomely congratulates Charles on his litigation successes of the prior year, and then, almost as an afterthought, expresses a concern about his pro bono work. "Usually, we discuss pro bono with someone at the firm first, Charles," says Henry. "Some of the partners have been disturbed that you haven't done that."

Charles instantly gets his back up and goes on the attack. He accuses his fellow lawyers en masse of insensitivity to charitable issues and shortsightedness regarding the firm's image. In the face of overall praise for his good work and a sensible suggestion about the need to pull together as colleagues, Charles hears only a criticism. He reads the professional advice as a challenge and turns a prideful moment into an unpleasant confrontation.

Like most ambivalents, this man has trouble accepting support. It's difficult for him to be a team player who will take into account the concerns and feelings of others, although he's quick to voice his own. Most especially, he reacts poorly to limit setting, or any hint of being told what to do.

That tendency to take over and be in charge gets the ambivalent into trouble in his marriage or long-term love relationship. This is an individual with only the haziest notion of personal boundaries, of what's involved in respecting a partner's sense of privacy, and of how to refrain from being inappropriately invasive. He'll feel free to intrude upon his partner's time, friendships, activities, possessions, or thoughts. The distinction between "yours, mine, and ours" doesn't come easily to him, nor does the need to let go of the kind of mundane interference that can drive a love partner up the wall, or out the door.

• **impatient.** The ambivalent suffers from a pervading lack of patience when going through life's inevitable processes.

Consider Mel and his girlfriend, preparing for a drive to the country and some cycling. When Mel attempts to hook the bike rack to the car, he can't get it to work, and suddenly shouts: "Polly, get over here and help me, I can't get this damn thing up." Polly says: "Okay, calm down, let's see how it goes." She, too, is unsuccessful at attaching the rack to the car, whereupon Mel gets even madder: "Goddammit, that's all screwed up, just leave it." Polly walks off. Mel throws the bike rack on the ground and goes to get a beer.

He's irritated that she can't do what he couldn't do in the first place, and feels foolish, which makes him become even angrier. So he attacks her for her inadequacy. Patience is not on the ambivalent's list of virtues.

- **critical.** Because she knows her way is best or because she's compelled to express her own feelings and turn a deaf ear to those of others, the ambivalent has a hard time solving relationship problems, even when she wants to.

Angela's critical mode comes to the surface, for example, when she pays a visit to her parents, who are spending their retirement years delightedly going off to see the world. Whenever Angela returns home for a Sunday afternoon or a weekend visit, her mother and father are eager to discuss plans for their upcoming tour of China or show her snapshots from their recent trip to South America. Every time she is on her way to their house, Angela resolves to be "nice" that day. She plans to show interest and attempt to share some of the pleasure her parents are taking in their travels—because she really does wish to be closer to them. Some bad feelings have popped up and then dissipated in past years, and she desires a more peaceful and adult level of communication. Each time, she fails.

Within an hour, Angela can't maintain her resolve, and she voices her opinion that packaged tours, besides being excessively costly, don't give anyone a real taste of foreign countries. She merely glances at the itinerary for the next trip, remarks, "Well, this is certainly one of those 'If today is Tuesday we must be in Belgium' deals." On one recent visit, Angela's fiancé, Joe, joins her, and makes all the right interested, or at least polite, comments. This only serves to raise her hackles and sets her to picking at Joe later, accusing him of being a "suck-up."

• **volatile.** He overreacts or underreacts. He's oppressively close, and then, almost without warning, remote. The ambivalent often wants the feelings and moods of the moment, his partner's and his own, to be different from what they are. When he can't make that happen, he becomes frustrated, anxious, and contentious.

That volatility, paradoxically, is the means by which the ambivalent maintains a sense of equilibrium. Settling into an ongoing, reasoned kind of interaction makes this individual nervous. He's desirous of, and capable of, *short-term* stability— a romance or a friendship might run smoothly for six months, then it's off for three months, because he'll sabotage it.

• **desirous of comfort and support, but can't accept it.** Janice, a sophomore in college, gets into an intensely unpleasant bit of business with her roommate, who wrongfully accuses Janice of stealing some of her research notes for a term paper. The matter escalates to a meeting with the dean of students and ends in an unsatisfactory resolution, all of which makes Janice upset. She seethes and feels very alone. When her boyfriend arrives on campus the next day for a date, Janice starts to tell him about the incident, then bursts into tears and rails at him for his lack of understanding and sympathy.

One would expect this young woman to obtain a measure of comfort and calm from the appearance of someone who's dear to her, but this is not so. To the contrary, her boyfriend's presence seems to add to her stress and anxiousness and make her feel even worse. Ambivalents like Janice have learned over time that support is an iffy business, and that a loved one cannot always be trusted to supply it. They want it, but can't accept it.

• **antsy in groups, and prefers one-to-one relationships.**
Ellen and Jim, dating for about four months, join Jim's
friends Tom and Alice in a little beach volleyball. The object
is an afternoon of relaxation and fun, since none of them
are especially good at the game. Ellen at once establishes a
set of rules, chastises the others for infractions, then herself
hits the ball any way she wants. With the fun evaporating
fast, the game breaks up quickly and everyone retreats to
their blankets, where Ellen snuggles up to Jim and seductively applies sunblock to his back.

Ellen is not actually antisocial. She enters situations involving other people, but once there, does little to try to fit
in or adapt. This is a starkly ambivalent bit of behavior.

Accepted into the group, the ambivalent gets anxious and
wants out, perhaps inappropriately and noticeably going off
by herself. One of two reactions may ensue: People get dis-
gusted with her moody, ungiving behavior and feel angry
toward her, or they try to be exceptionally kind and wel-
coming, to draw her back in. Either way, the ambivalent
manages to focus attention on herself and get the group to
come to her.

• **sexy.** Bob describes his new girlfriend, Kirsten, as "the
sexiest woman I've ever met." She's vivacious, lively, unpredictable, moody—"a thoroughly maddening individual," he
says, "but she comes on to me in the most remarkable ways.
I've never been with a woman who so outrageously flirts
with me! It's irresistible."

Like many ambivalents, Kirsten apparently sends out
strong sexual vibes and enjoys that aspect of her personality.
Sex is often what keeps an ambivalent's relationship going.

• **upset by separations, and responds to them angrily.**
When Amanda learns her clothing manufacturing firm is

sending her on a two-week buying trip to India and Turkey, she's over the moon. She'd been pushing for the trip for half a year, and has a notebook full of sources and ideas she wants to explore. Her boyfriend, Tim, is thrilled for her, and enjoys listening to her plans. As the day of departure approaches, however, Amanda becomes excessively jittery and jerky with Tim. She curtly cancels a date to meet after work, then calls him in the middle of the night, desperate to talk.

The evening before she leaves, they have a blowout battle, precipitated by Tim's casual remark that she should check her return flight plans to see how far in advance they would need to be changed, in case she elects to stay overseas a few days longer. Amanda accuses Tim of wanting to see her go; he replies that she's acting like an idiot, gives her a kiss, and says goodbye.

Ambivalent Amanda doesn't handle separations well. On one hand, she's delighted about her trip and expects it to be exciting, productive, and fun. On the other hand, she's terribly afraid to leave, because she's uncertain what or whom she'll find when she returns. Enjoyment of her independence is dulled by the anxiety of separation.

• **quick to place blame.** The ambivalent either adores or hates her partner or friends at any given moment. Establishing consistent, even relationships is difficult; when something goes awry, she's quick to put the blame elsewhere.

When Jennifer's closest friend Ellie takes a job in another city, Jennifer can't wait to pay her a visit. Ellie takes her time—too much time, Jennifer thinks—getting established in a new apartment and new workplace. Jennifer calls her friend almost daily, and finally a visit is arranged. But Jennifer doesn't have a good time. Ellie wants to show her the local sights, but Jennifer wants to "hang" and have some of their long talks. At one point, Ellie takes a chatty phone call from a co-worker, much to Jennifer's annoyance. When Ellie wants her to meet some of her new friends over dinner, Jennifer is further annoyed over having to share this special time with others. Back home, Jennifer complains about her friend's "immaturity" and doesn't return Ellie's phone messages. The friendship is on hold, maybe dead.

It's not an atypical scenario for the ambivalent, whose friendships frequently break up because negative experiences are seen as the fault of others; lost relationships are then easily forgotten. Talking about a former pal or connection, the ambivalent may find it difficult to integrate a range of feelings into a smooth story and full picture. Her memories have themes of betrayal; if she is betrayed, she can devalue the past relationship and continue without feeling the loss.

• **a "terrible two" at times.** As we have noted, the ambivalent reacts badly to any hint of limit setting. When he doesn't get his way, he's quite capable of throwing a grown-up tantrum.

Jeff, a successful literary agent, repeatedly accepts evening engagements for himself and his fiancée, Nina, without consulting her first. When Nina's own job pressures prevent her from joining him, Jeff responds angrily, either slamming down the phone or storming out the door. Because he has difficulty trusting that Nina's unavailability has nothing to do with him, he feels rejected and gets angry.

Those tantrums and fights all go to the issue of autonomy, a big problem for the ambivalent. He proves to himself his strength, his autonomy, and his worthiness to be loved by besting or overwhelming the other person.

• **a seductive maker-upper.** When the ambivalent has pushed his partner or friend a little too long and hard and he's suddenly feeling remorseful about the temper tantrum, he leaps into action.

After behaving like a "terrible two," for example, Jeff will become excessively loving toward Nina to win her back over, with little regard for how she's feeling about his recent tantrum or little thought that she might value a bit of distance as she thinks over the outburst. The ambivalent's talent at a quick, often sexual reconnecting can be a challenge for his partner, one of the pleasures and pitfalls of forging a long-term relationship.

• **a fool for love.** She falls in love quickly. If she's unattached, she's sure that each new romantic relationship will be the one and only. She will ignore potential or obvious problems. When the object of her attention gets too close or, on the other hand, fails to offer the unconditional love she seeks, she pushes him away. Throughout her maneuvers in finding romance, she focuses on how she is "being loved" by the other, not on how she is loving.

But when she has found (she thinks) Mr. Right, she marshals all her emotional energy, all her persuasive powers, to pull him to her. She's single-mindedly set on making the catch, and even capable of keying down her own excessive behavior until she succeeds. Then she's not so interested any longer.

In romance, the ambivalent's push-pull behavior comes galloping to the fore, making it hard for her to adopt a reliable strategy for achieving the love and affection she seeks. She's there, and then not quite there. We might call Emma, in Flaubert's *Madame Bovary*, the quintessential ambivalent-in-love. Courting Charles, Emma is "animated one moment, her eyes wide and innocent, then half closed, her gaze clouding with boredom, her thoughts drifting." Although she makes her catch, Emma is soon disenchanted, reflecting that once she "had thought she was in love; but since she lacked the happiness that should have come from that love, she must have been mistaken."

Disappointed in romance, the ambivalent is often drawn to unavailable people, who prove her right in her anticipation of dissatisfaction. She may look for love in all the wrong places and confuse sex with intimacy. Both ambivalent men and women are more apt to have romances with married people than are secures or avoidants.

More than anything, this individual wants to experience unconditional love, to be aligned with the other, who will satisfy all needs. A woman with an ambivalent attachment style may fantasize that having a baby will provide her with such unconditional love. In her unrealistic expectations, however, she may also intend to be pregnant, thin, and glamorous all at the same time.

An impossible character? The flip side to the push-pull nature of ambivalent attachment and the overall intensity of emotion it fosters accounts for much of the ambivalent's appeal and strength.

As we will see in the chapters in Part III, the ambivalent can be a charming, loving, even useful partner to the more reasoned secure or the more remote avoidant, adding a measure of spice or a needed dose of emotion to daily life.

Couple Fits

YOU meet, you fall in love, you become a couple. In the earliest stages of togetherness, you can seem a world unto yourselves, exchanging languorous glances, slow smiles, and shorthand talk that send messages only you two understand. Amid a gaggle of friends or family, you emit those slightly exclusionary vibes that tell the world, *We've got something going on here that no one else can be part of.*

Just like a mother and her child. With all that absorption in and communication with each other, two lovers are in the process of reenacting their wish to merge—to join another in an intimate union, just as each once was in infancy. Deeply embedded in each, but temporarily muted, lies the predominant style of attachment learned back in the cradle from that original love partner.

Flash forward a bit. Some of the "in love" flavor has faded; you've settled into "a relationship" now. The differences between you that you once hardly noticed or found adorable sprout up as little pockets of annoyance or as potentially larger problems. In wrestling with jobs, money, sex, friends, relatives, kids, and chores, and all the routine stresses of an ongoing intimate relationship, your predominant attachment style and your partner's find many opportunities to surface. Caught off guard at times by your behaviors, you wonder: Where is *that* coming from? Why am I acting this way? Why is my partner acting that way? What's going on here? Maybe you wonder: Was this whole thing a big mistake?

What's going on, in fact, reflects the inescapable unfolding of the couple fit. Intimate relationships activate a central aspect of attachment behavior: the need to negotiate the emotional, mental, and physical separation each partner can tolerate, the distance at which each feels a maximum of support and a minimum of frustration and anxiety. Negotiating distance involves setting comfortable psychological, mental, and physical boundaries or levels of privacy. And for each partner, as we've seen, whether he or she has started out in life as secure, avoidant, or ambivalent is going to determine just how those boundaries are drawn.

The secure can handle a hefty degree of distance *and* intimacy. She lets her partner know what she expects and doesn't fly into a rage or panic if those expectations come up short. The avoidant, loath to share her deepest thoughts and feelings, prefers to keep her partner at a certain arm's length. She looks in the other direction when that partner gets too close for comfort. The ambivalent, who dislikes rules and expectations, demands privacy and distance one moment, and violates it the next.

So, put two attachment styles together and what happens? An easygoing relationship between two secures is going to be very different from a relationship between two ambivalents—a coupling that crackles with the charge produced by explosive emotions and a lack of many boundaries at all—and also very different from a relationship between two avoidants, where a remote quietude may prevail.

Put a secure together with an avoidant, and will one partner be doing the emotional work of two? In the ambivalent/avoidant pair, is one mate's impulsivity likely to drive the other underground or out the door?

In chapters 7 through 12, we're going to step inside each of the six relationship combinations, following a number of couples as they hammer out a better fit. But before we lead you into the thick of things with each of our significant pairs, we invite you to listen in to some revealing conversations.

THE HE/SHE DIALOGUES: EVELYN AND SHEILA'S *COUPLE FITS* SURVEY

For the purposes of fleshing out our own understanding of attachment styles and how they are demonstrated within intimate relationships, we interviewed and then videotaped several dozen volunteer couples (about two-thirds were married; one-third were involved in serious relationships of varying lengths). Each couple willingly gave up an hour of their time to participate in our survey.

To start, each pair filled out several questionnaires, separately—that is, he answered his and she answered hers. The questionnaires, essentially a quiz similar to the one you completed earlier, were designed to let us know how each individual felt about his or her intimate attachments, especially what each thought about the marriage or the relationship in which they were currently involved.

We asked some questions about how this man or woman would describe his or her parent, way back when, in terms of her availability and willingness to offer comfort and soothing.

Our subjects were then asked to move a little further along in the chronological memory bank, and reflect on the most important romances they had been involved in—were they trusting, jealous a lot of the time, wildly or mildly attracted, mostly happy or unhappy?

Finally, we touched on the nitty-gritty of today. We hoped to come up with the hot spots for this pair as a pair, the areas in which one or both found the highest degree of dissatisfaction or revealed the greatest difference in point of view. On a scale of 1 (always agree) to 6 (always disagree), each reported on the degree of harmony in their relationship regarding finances, leisure time, demonstrations of affection, friends, sexual relations, and several other items. We asked a couple of big questions: If you had your life to live over, would you marry the same person, marry a different person, or not marry at all? Do you confide in your mate almost never, rarely, in most things, or in everything?

Our volunteers looked through a list of about three dozen items and weighed in on whether they would like their partner to do less or more in some of these areas—prepare interesting meals, take me out for some more fun, get together with my relatives, show appreciation for the things I do, have more sex or less, argue with me, pay the bills, spend more time with me, leave me more time to myself, and so on.

Those last answers gave us the ideas we needed to write up for each couple a tailor-made script, as it were, for their videotaped session. In fact, this was not so much a script as a list of key words or ideas for an improvisational actor.

Whenever we spotted extreme questionnaire responses, of the "strongly disagree" or "want lots more of" variety, and especially when one partner's answer differed dramatically from the other's, we knew these two would have—or *should* have—lots to talk about. If neither indicated much wish for change or dissatisfaction over "spending time with relatives" or "keeping the house neat," for example, we believed that those issues wouldn't stir things up. And what we wanted, of course, was to stir things up—to see how this couple addressed an uncomfortable area and how they revealed that discomfort to each other, how or whether they listened or heard each other, how or whether they moved closer to compromise or resolution.

We gave each couple a piece of paper on which we had written:

"Please discuss all of the following topics, or any number you choose. Please continue talking for ten minutes. You may discuss as many or as few of these topics as you wish." We listed up to six items that, based on the questionnaire responses, we anticipated would get them going, in ways that showed their attachment styles at work.

We sat them down, rolled our videotape, and left them alone for those ten minutes. When time was up, we went back in and told the couple to take a little break, go outside and walk around, get a cup of coffee, do whatever. And then, as the final assignment, they were brought back into their room, with the videotape rolling, and instructed to talk for five minutes about anything they wished.

You may recall our earlier descriptions of the Strange Situation Test, in which the young, preverbal child and his parent spend time together in an unfamiliar place, then are separated, then are reunited. If so, you may recognize in our survey a similar setup of an adult variety. In getting our couples together to talk, breaking up the talk, and then reuniting them, we replicated to some extent those controlled mother/child experiments that showed vividly the behaviors of the secure, avoidant, and ambivalent youngster toward the object of his most powerful love.

When all was done and our couples had gone home, we sat down with our questionnaires and tapes and a small team of counselors who understood attachment theory and shared our sense of it as a powerful couples dynamic. From their questionnaire responses, we "diagnosed" each individual as one of the three types—secure, ambivalent, or avoidant. Then we watched our tapes.

Although several of our respondents had themselves pegged pretty well, most did not. What we saw and heard in their interactions demonstrated how difficult it usually is for a woman and a man to understand how they search to make connection, to feel comfortably close. The intellectual self-analysis—yes, I'm an open person, I can handle things, I appreciate my partner's different point of view—often did not jibe with the voices, looks, and attitudes that the individual displayed.

We've selected from our store of "controlled experiments" several tapes that are good representations of the six pair combinations: the secure/secure couple, the secure/avoidant couple, the secure/ambivalent couple, the avoidant/avoidant couple, the avoidant/ambivalent couple, and the ambivalent/ambivalent couple. We start off each of the following chapters with an abbreviated transcript of what transpired between each pair as they tackled their assignment. Not so surprisingly, most of our couples indicated the same "hot spot" issues—money, sex, kids, affection, and appreciation, the matters we all wrestle with. For each, we report only the words we heard and the actions we watched. We give here no other information—what jobs they have, where they live, how old their kids are, how long they've been together. We give them no names, just "he" and "she."

Listen, and see what you can hear. Read how we size up the attachment style revelations. Get a general picture of the styles at work. Reflect on the difficulty we all have expressing ourselves in the words and actions that have the best chance of bringing us closer to a partner in love and understanding—for therein lies the essence of negotiating a better fit.

TOWARD A MORE COMFORTABLE COUPLE FIT

From there, we proceed to our case histories, and explore more detailed examples. Each pair we describe is based on a particular couple or couples we have counseled, with identifying specifics disguised or modified for privacy's sake. For each, we reveal what goes right—what can be appealing, exciting, supportive, or functional between the two—and what goes wrong—what causes disappointments, storms, or misunderstandings. We also outline the goals—what each individual must do to move toward workable adjustments or temporary negotiations.

If you know by now where you and your beloved fit in the attachment scheme of things, we are confident you'll uncover in these couples' stories some striking parallels to your own experiences. And we're confident that you'll take away from the lessons of these partners some ideas on how to achieve more of the good stuff and less of the bad stuff in the daily dealings and long-term prospects of your relationship.

Those ideas we might call the homework or the assignments you will put to use, *to the extent you find possible*.

Most of the couples who come to us for counseling find it not so difficult to sit in the relative calm of the therapist's office and practice telling each other, "I really would like more XYZ from you," or, "I think you're good at ABC and I'm better at DEF, so let's try not to get in an argument about that next time." On their own, however, many of them run into trouble implementing those actions. Often, then, we'll suggest that a couple who have achieved a fair degree of insight and indicated a willingness to keep renegotiating the fit come back to talk a bit more and return for a touchup once a month or once every other month. Gradually, they find the new, intentional, improved behaviors easier to sustain.

The point of all this for you to remember is this: The

"homework assignments" or recommendations that follow are good goals to shoot for, not magical and certainly not instant solutions. If some of them work for you some of the time, you're moving forward. Think in terms of those workable adjustments and temporary negotiations, gradual shifts in habitual ways of acting or reacting that effectively introduce greater accommodation and acceptance into your couple fit. Getting down to the depths is not necessarily required to promote and enjoy a much more satisfactory, more comfortable relationship. As counselors who have worked with hundreds of couples over the years, however, we can say with absolute conviction that examining your attachment style— what we'll often refer to in the following pages as your "passion"—certainly can allow for deep exploration and understanding, as well as resolution.

Are you living with a partner who expresses no interest in any of this? You think he's the least likely human on the planet to read "his" side of the homework and say, "Hmm, yes, I see now what I have to do." Do it for him. You will, we guarantee, find ways to push your resistant partner a bit out of character and to extract from him some small changes that will make your life pleasanter and get you further along the path.

CHAPTER 7

Cuing In:
The Secure/Secure Couple

HE AND SHE

He and she settle into their chairs, take a look at our list of topics, and jointly decide that "Getting angry" is a good place to start:

HE: Okay, let's see, getting angry . . . I don't get angry. I can't recall ever getting really angry with you since we've been married. *(He laughs.)* I'd say I have a problem here—a chronic inability to become angry. What do you think, is there something wrong with me?

SHE: No. It's wonderful. In fact, it's an absolute miracle! *(They both laugh.)*

But I'd say I do have a problem with anger. It's hard for me to get angry; it sort of builds up over time . . . and then it's difficult for me to get over it.

Instead of just getting it right out in the open, I worry it around for too long.

HE: Um-hmm. Well, I have to say you're so good to me that I've really had nothing to get angry about—except maybe my mother. *(They both smile.)* When she was more . . .

SHE: When she was more her usual self.

(They talk about a problem that has clearly given this couple grief over time, the often unpleasant presence of his mother in their joint lives. His mother, it emerges, is now an elderly woman, "not entirely herself anymore," so some of the storms have died down.)

SHE: I used to get so angry with her. She could make life pretty miserable for us, you must admit. The wonderful thing is that somehow through all that, we were able to stay together and to work out a very happy life together.

HE: Yes, we've done that, very well I'd say. So, what about me makes you mad? Do you get angry with me and not tell me?

SHE *(with a chuckle)*: Very, very seldom! Of course, I'll get bothered by something every now and then, but I don't feel good when I get you upset. I'll usually wait until I'm very sure of how to express what I want to say, and then I always watch you very carefully! If I see your lips are getting stretched thin over your teeth, I think, Uh-oh, and I back off! But if I still think I have a case, I'll come back to you later on and pursue it. I think overall we've been pretty good at hashing things out.

HE: Agree. I do the same thing, I suppose. If I have something I know you'd just as soon not hear, I put some thought into figuring out how to phrase it as kindly as possible!

Well, let's see, what next? What are you going to do tomorrow with the kids [their grandchildren]? Could you stop by my mother's and let them visit for a while? It does mean a lot to her now to see them.

SHE: I'll see how the day shapes up. It'll depend on when your mother is napping and where I'm taking the kids for lunch, and if the timing is right we'll stop in.

You know, thinking about this further, the thing about your mother . . . The only times I've felt abandoned, in a sense, were when I felt you didn't grasp what was going on, what she was doing and how really hurtful she could be. While I was struggling with that, you were telling me, essentially, "Just ignore her, just forget about it."

HE: I know that's true, because the way I learned to deal with her a long time ago was just to tune her out, and not pay much attention to her opinions, not pay emotional attention . . . because I realized she needed to be right all the time, whether she was or not. When she said something critical, I'd consider the source it was coming from and just shrug it off. So I guess I didn't see why anybody else should worry about it either or take her too seriously.

SHE: Well, I think now, after the passage of all these years, you probably were right. You dealt with her in the best way. But it turned out that I didn't know how to deal with her at all. This was something that in my own family I hadn't encountered, and it was different and difficult. And for so long I simply did not know what to do about her.

HE: Um-hum. And I didn't know what to do about that. You know, I think the reason I don't get very angry in general is because I learned as a child, from her really, that it didn't get me anywhere. It just got me into more trouble, more punishment, so I figured out other ways of reacting to problems—maybe analyzing them or some other approach. And I found out I could manage my affairs without getting angry, maybe by always taking the analytical view of what was happening, so to speak.

SHE: And I think you were successful at that. You hit on the right solution for yourself. On the other hand, I had to find the right solution for me regarding your mother, one that I could live with. Eventually what happened, I think, was that I made a decision to deal with these issues in my way, without bringing them to you all the time.

HE: And what strategy did you develop?

(They laugh.)

SHE: Well, I wouldn't call it a full-blown strategy. But I felt that I had to confront her and I learned to do that. When she would say something hurtful or would act with the children in a way I found unacceptable, I didn't let it pass. I confronted her, talked to her and told her my feelings on the score.

HE: I know you've done that. And you've been right on target about it. That was the right approach for you.

(Their ten minutes are up. Later, the reconciliation.)

HE: We can talk about anything? Well, I'd actually like to talk about that leak. How's that for a subject? I think it's got to be at the head of our agenda now. I'm thinking of a plastic tarp temporarily over that window area to keep the water out, and then I'll take the clay out of the window well, put in more gravel, clean the pipe.

SHE: See, the thing that continues to worry me is that we may need to re-tar the roof. And if that's the case, this repair won't work. We could come back from vacation and find a flood.

HE: That's a possibility, but I think the risk of that is relatively small.

SHE: I feel differently about this, as you know, but I'll go along with you. And that fellow who came to check the drains seemed to agree with you.

HE: On the other hand, if you feel so strongly about getting a new roof that you're willing to give up five years of birthday and anniversary presents in order to pay for it, as you told me the other night . . .

SHE (*laughing*): Well, I did say I'd sign a document to that effect.

HE: Well, look, if spending a couple of thousand on the roof will keep you happy, let's do it and get it done with.

SHE: The trouble with signing a document is that you know and I know if it's something I really want, you'll agree and give it to me. So the document isn't going to work.

HE: True enough.

SHE: We could agree that we won't take a vacation next year, and we'll put that money on the roof. And we'll both sign a document! But would we stick to it? Look, I think you really want to try your idea about the drains, and prove to yourself that it has merit, and that's all right. If we get back home to a flood, we'll deal with that.

(*The counselor comes in to say time's up.*)

It's not hard to spot elements of the securely attached couple in these two, starting with body language, which, of course, speaks volumes. He and she are a "proper," almost formal-seeming pair, who dress elegantly and sit up straight in their respective chairs! At the same time, they give off an air of relaxation and comfort; each looks intently at the other as he or she talks, their bodies slightly inclined toward each other in an unconscious demonstration of acceptance. The frequent "Um-hums," nods, chuckles, and smiles are further indications that these two are really listening and paying attention to the conversation. There are encouragements as well, the small cues by which one partner says, in effect, "Go on, I hear you, I understand what you're saying, it's safe to speak your mind here." While their interaction has little "oomph" to it, there is no sign that either would like more energetic or emotional responses from the other.

Significantly but not surprisingly, at no point does either partner get into chapter and verse about just what that disagreeable mother/mother-in-law actually did to make life tough for them. Other than the broad suggestions that she could be equally critical of her son and her daughter-in-law and say "hurtful" things, they make no reference to specific offenses.

Was she a screamer and a shouter? A demander of impossible attention? A crafty manipulator of affections? We're curious, but this couple has no need to rehash old stories; they both know and accept Mom's sins. He doesn't get his back up and come to his mother's defense; he's on his partner's side. She doesn't shy away from calling a spade a spade and naming Mom as the sometime thorn in their marriage, but it's clear that she's on her partner's side too. Each sees no payoff in retreading that old ground, and has the ability to focus on a more critical issue—how each has come to "handle" Mom. And then, what to do about that roof.

BILL AND SANDRA

Sandra, an HMO administrator, and Bill, an accountant, have been married for a year and a half. It's the second marriage for both. Bill, a quiet man with an easy smile and a droll manner, is stepfather to Sandra's two early-teens children.

She's a lively woman who gestures animatedly with her hands as she describes what has brought them for counseling: "There have been a lot of adjustments for both of us, but we've worked things out pretty well, except for two ongoing issues—my kids and his brother! Bill is great with my children, and they're crazy about him. But he thinks I give them too much attention. He wants more of me. And I could do with a whole lot less of his brother, who's a walking wounded."

Bill agrees: "My brother is difficult. He's always got problems, always needs something, shows up at our place at odd times. He's had some issues with booze and drugs in the past. Not to mention money."

Sandra has been struggling with the pull of time with Bill versus time with her children. She recognizes that, appropriately, her husband wants to feel he is her star. And she says she thinks Bill is probably right when he tells her she's overinvolved with the kids' schoolwork, schedules, and extracurricular activities. For his part, Bill has been trying to take a tougher stand with his brother: "I had a no-holds-barred talk with him recently, and I told him if he wanted to maintain a relationship with Sandra and me and continue to be welcome in our lives, we've got to agree on some ground rules and limits." Recently, though, Bill has spent several weekends in a row helping his brother get set up in a new apartment, to Sandra's annoyance.

Neither is a stranger to conflict and confrontation. Bill and Sandra each initiated divorce from their respective first spouses. Bill's former wife, he tells us, gradually withdrew from him sexually and eventually revealed she had had an affair with a co-worker, a romance she had since ended. "That was it as far as I was concerned," he says now. "I talked it out with her, but she didn't seem to grasp the profoundness of what had happened, at least in my mind. There was no way to pull back together as a couple after that kind of lying and sneakiness." Sandra's ex-husband, a salesman, was on the road most of the time during their ten-year marriage and developed a gambling problem, of which she was largely unaware until she discovered that a savings account earmarked for college tuitions had been emptied. About that point, Sandra decided she and the kids needed to leave.

In the process of working into their new couple fit, Bill and Sandra haven't yet figured out how to integrate those "outsiders"—her children and his brother—into their unit. Each one's sensitivity to the responsibilities that take them away from themselves as a couple, and their feelings about those separations, is probably partially a fallout of the fact that each has come from a failed marriage. But they see what's going on; they've put those issues on the table.

ANNIE AND JAY

Annie and Jay have been living together for four years, having fallen in love and joined forces shortly after they met as junior staffers at a Washington, D.C., TV station. She's thirty-eight, he's thirty-six. Perfectly content with their arrangement and unpressured by either family, they've seen little reason to get married. "The piece of paper has never resonated with us a whole lot," says Annie. "We're committed to each other." Lately, for a couple of reasons, she and Jay have been giving some thought to what that commitment should entail.

Annie has climbed a media ladder, from researcher to on-air news reader to her current position as a field reporter, which has required her to spend a total of probably two or three months out of the year on far-flung assignments. Living out of a suitcase, charging out to catch a plane on an hour's notice, and decompressing back home again, has suited her. "I love my job, love the pace," she says, "but it's not a life I want to live forever."

Her schedule and their romantic, fun-filled reconnections have suited Jay, too. He thinks she's fantastic—"a dynamo, so full of enthusiasm for everything, the most exciting woman I've ever known." He admires her ability to land on the other side of the globe and do a tough job, and loves hearing her stories later. And he keeps his own busy schedule running a specialized travel and guide agency for people craving the unusual in outdoor adventure. When time has allowed, they've enjoyed taking off on mini-adventures of their own. "Jay has actually won me over to the pleasures of backpacking and scuba diving. Even rock climbing, a thing I would never in my wildest dreams have thought was my cup of tea!" says Annie. She thinks he's pretty fantastic too, "and a smart businessman—I like that about him."

So, why the sudden interest in marriage? we ask. "Well, as a woman pushing forty, I can say I'd like to have a baby sometime before I'm fifty," Annie says, "and I think a child should have a husband and wife as parents." Jay indicates he also likes the idea of starting a family.

One issue on the agenda: Jay is Jewish and Annie is Episcopalian, "both fairly well lapsed," they say. But if they do get married, Annie would like the church wedding now, "especially for my mother, but for me too." No problem with Jay. Thinking, hopefully, about the future children who have inspired this marriage talk, however, both have strong ideas about their religions, somewhat to their surprise. He'd like any offspring to be raised in the Jewish tradition; Annie isn't sure she's comfortable with that idea.

Besides that, they admit to some cold feet about getting the piece of paper. "I don't want the zing to go out of our relationship," says Annie. "Some of the passion goes when it gets official. We've seen this with some of our friends. Life gets flat. One couple we know very well is now separated, three years after the wedding."

Jay was the one who suggested they come for counseling, to air with a therapist these issues over which they've been having many late-night talk sessions themselves.

MILLIE AND MICHAEL

They met in college at a student rally protesting the administration's failure to appoint as dean a much admired though controversial female professor. In the early years of their marriage, they worked together for abortion rights, education funding, environmental protection—"your stereotypical do-gooder liberals out in the trenches," says Michael.

Now in their late forties, married for almost twenty-five years, Millie and Michael have followed largely parallel paths for a long time. "I'm still in the trenches, he's on the podium," is how Millie puts it. "He's got a closet full of dinner suits and a tux, I've got a drawer full of jeans and paint-splattered sweatshirts."

Both remain passionately committed to the issues they

consider important, but they've lived out that commitment in different venues. Over the past ten or twelve years, Millie has become deeply involved in the concerns of imprisoned women, and spends virtually every day working with mothers serving jail terms at a local penitentary. "We help them learn computer skills, and we've started a library and a playroom where they can spend time with their kids," she says. "I'm happiest at one-on-one efforts, establishing a connection with someone over time and seeing the difference I can make in that person's life."

Michael, on the other hand, decided years ago to apply his energies at the policymaking and fund-raising levels, and discovered, somewhat to his surprise, that he loved the relative limelight. "I'm good at it," he says, "I can get out there and make speeches, drum up money, bring together the people we need." What he does involves a fair amount of traveling, frequent official dinners, and glamorous, big-ticket evening events—almost none of which Millie has attended with him.

"I guess we evolved an understanding gradually," she says, and he nods in agreement. "He does his thing, I do my thing. But we have the same core values." Neither has ever been especially interested in making money, for example, and they're grateful that small but comfortable family inheritances on both sides have enabled them to pursue their chosen paths. They believe ferociously that marriage must encompass the freedom and independence of each partner if it is to thrive. And they have been mutually devoted to their four children—"three of them any parent's dream and one of them the nightmare," says Michael, as Millie looks away with a wince at that harsh word.

Their youngest child, sixteen-year-old Molly, has been skating on thin ice for a long time—skipping school, doing drugs, and often lying to her parents about where she's going and with whom. Michael and Millie have had different thoughts on the what-to-do-about-Molly issue. He's been inclined to come down hard, set strict limits and serious consequences for bad behavior, but for the past year he's agreed to back off and follow Millie's gentler approach. Deciding he needed to carve out more time at home, he cut back his evening activities drastically. Both parents, together and separately, have had long walks and talks with their daughter, worked hard at understanding her feelings, and given her leeway in an effort to convince her of their trust and confidence.

"That way hasn't worked," Michael says now. Molly's running wilder than ever. One recent afternoon, Millie returned home to find a message on their answering machine, requesting that she come to the local precinct, where Molly was being held for possession of drugs. Now Michael has swung into action, arranging interviews at a residential school-cum-treatment center for troubled youngsters.

Millie's distressed: "This place is in another state. Molly would be there for two years, during which she'd essentially be locked on the grounds. We wouldn't even be able to visit her during the first year."

Michael and Millie are on to their first serious rupture over the matter of how to help their daughter.

Bill and Sandra, Annie and Jay, and Millie and Michael, just like our He and She couple who introduced this chapter, display characteristics of the secure/secure pair, a connection rooted in mutual and generally thoughtful responsiveness. As each of these couples sit in our office and talk about their relationship and matters of concern, they look at each other, from time to time reaching out to touch in order to emphasize a point or show understanding. Conversation flows, even when the talk gets heated. Bill and Sandra, for example, accept each other's expressed complaints—his brother, her kids—as legitimate, without demanding "proof." And clearly, they're willing to take on issues that inescapably involve conflict and confrontation.

The secure/secure married pair have provided the heart of many traditional television situation comedies, from *Ozzie and Harriet* to *The Cosby Show* to *Mad About You*. Right from their start as a couple, for example, Paul and Jamie Buchman of *Mad About You* had their differences and fights—he wanted to hold on to his old bachelor apartment, she wanted to hold on to her old boyfriend's T-shirts; he didn't want to buy a couch because it meant "commitment," she walked off and shopped alone. But their struggles were always in the service of working things out and keeping the relationship going. Although it wasn't always easy, they worked at understanding where the other was "coming from."

Two secures do have a fine capacity for empathy. They can put themselves in the other's place, without losing sight of their own interests and needs. They can talk about insecurities and not feel vulnerable or diminished, and small arguments don't escalate into World War III.

During a disagreement, each is motivated to discuss and understand rather than to dominate and control and be seen as "right." When Michael went along with his partner's conviction that allowing their daughter greater freedom might reduce the destructive behavior, and the approach backfired, he didn't pin blame on Millie. "That way didn't work," he says, simply and accurately, and it's time to try something else. He does not call their initial approach "Millie's way" or say "her cockeyed ideas about discipline were a disaster."

The unsatisfactory prior marriages Bill and Sandra described, and what each did about them, reveal two other significant aspects to the secure attachment pattern. Secures can make bad judgments, like picking the wrong people. Because they interact, they are available and usually devoid of paranoia, and they can be a bit naive. But, when certain in their own minds that the relationship is untenable, and that no further talking or greater understanding can repair the damage, they'll usually move to end it. Dishonesty or any serious breach of trust is generally unacceptable to the secure, who'll make a clean, surgical break.

When it's time to go, in other words, he or she goes—unlike avoidants who, fearful of losing their love objects, are capable of floundering on indefinitely in denial of an unhappy reality. And unlike ambivalents, who tend to threaten divorce, the secure, with a sturdy sense of self, doesn't threaten divorce, or drag on for years in couples therapy. He or she acts.

An added thought: Although Bill and Sandra showed the hallmarks of secure attachment with each other, a number of comments they made about their prior relationships—the fights, the painful upheavals, periods of denial followed by fresh disappointments—suggested to us that Bill had displayed an avoidant style and Sandra had displayed an ambivalent style back then. Now, each has evolved into the secure/secure fit. That's an occurrence we often see in second marriages. At least one partner has been through the wars, has learned hard lessons, feels stronger, craves true intimacy, and is ready to give up the fights. Life takes on more profound meanings. Each loses the passion to stay in the old fit, and shifts to a new passion for peace, stability, honesty, and greater comfort. Bill and Sandra's marriage, if we're right in our guesses about what went on before, demonstrates that attachment patterns can be fluid and evolving.

On the down side, two secures can be a mite too accommodating to each other. Always eager to forgive, forget, and restore the smooth-flowing life they enjoy, one may downplay a matter of personal importance. Unlike the avoidant, he's well in touch with his feelings on the score; he just finds it too easy to put them on the back burner in order to make up or get on with things. Each of our three couples needed to recognize the difference between genuinely agreeing to a course of action suggested by a partner, and simply accommodating or compromising.

We don't see many secure/secure couples in counseling, no doubt for the simple fact that this attachment style means they talk things over or argue them out when need be. They'll come to therapy around a specific issue or issues, often a biggie—serious business reversals, perhaps, or infidelity. Or, what do we need to do to get enough of each other and still take care of the other people in our lives? Or, should we get married? Or, how do we reach the right decision for our troubled child?

Overall, secure behavior works well as two partners search for answers. So the homework assignments for the secure/secure pair are few—but significant:

TOWARD A MORE COMFORTABLE COUPLE FIT

Recognize the Need for Agreement, Not Compromise, When That Need Arises

Or, we might say, be wary of an excess in your relationship of agreeing to disagree.

Secures, by and large, are pretty flexible people. Each partner wants to do what he or she can to make things work well, for both of them. Each is willing to try new approaches—the beauty of the secure/secure pair lies in that ability to appreciate the many ways to slice an apple and have it still taste like an apple. They're ready to cover for and help out the other, to say "yes" (our ambivalent will lead off with a "no"; the avoidant, with "What did you say?" or maybe, "We'll talk about that later"). Day-to-day living for this couple runs along in a generally easygoing, straightforward manner. Will you pick up the kids after school today? Okay if I meet you an hour later? How about ordering in Chinese tonight? All the ordinary bits of business involved in being together present few hassles.

Simple decisions get made simply: If one partner wants to see movie A and the other, movie B, one or the other is capable of saying, "Well, I'd prefer to go to this one but if you want to go to that one tonight, fine by me." Arguments that arise don't carry over. A decision on a matter at hand is just that, not an effort to rack up an emotional score—no "Let's see what I can extract from you" or "I'll go along with you this time, but then next time I'll get *my* way because now you owe me one." Secures don't keep those scores, and they're good at sticking to the issue. And if partner A makes the decision and takes the action and it turns out to be entirely wrong, partner B won't turn around and throw the disaster in the other's face. No little cracks. No attempts to undermine the partnership for future purposes. No tit-for-tat—"You sure as hell messed things up last time, so I guess I can mess things up this time."

That said, when two secures who are intelligent, self-confident, and articulate and possess strong feelings face a decision or crossroads, genuine agreement can be difficult. One might be likely to say, "Okay, I don't think so, but you do what you want and you take the responsibility for it." In other words, "I don't agree with you but I'll let you have your day in court." When the subject under discussion has relatively minor consequences—do we get a new roof or try an interim measure with the drains and the window?—not much is at stake. When the couple is faced with a weightier matter, though, the inability or unwillingness to agree might present problems.

As Annie and Jay discuss their children-to-be, it becomes clear that their religious differences, a matter of no significance to their day-to-day lives at the moment, may loom large in the future. "Nobody in my family is particularly observant," he says, "but all the kids—my brother, me, my cousins—got the training and the bar mitzvahs, and it's a part of my identity. I think as a kid you have to get that sense of connection to a tradition that's continued from previous generations." Annie remembers Sunday School classes and, with some nostalgia, participating in Christmas pageants and three-hour Good Friday services.

They're jumping the gun with this discussion of the appropriate religious education for their unborn children, says Annie with a smile. "Maybe we should both become Unitarians, how about that?" says Jay.

They do indeed have an abundance of time to work that one out, but as they negotiate this matter, and others that may arise about which each has strong feelings, we suggest it will be in their best interests to work toward reaching genuine agreements. A genuine agreement has about it the quality of wholehearted acceptance of and participation in a joint decision, even if that decision has required compromise on one side. If, for example, some day Annie takes their young son or daughter to church and Sunday School classes, and if Jay acquiesces, saying, in effect, "Go ahead, but I want no part of this," they will have merely agreed to disagree. If that kind of accommodation-without-agreement occurs in many areas of their joint life, therein lies the seed of conflict.

The secure/secure couple can go just so many times to that well, because eventually there's nothing left. Neither obtains what he or she really wants. They are in danger of emptying each other out, eroding the mutual value system or the groundwork for long-term growth, and losing a family or couple sense.

Millie and Michael pursue parallel interests in the world at large, share strong mutual values, and have a rich intimacy as well. They've fought for, and achieved, pretty much the exact life they want. So Molly, the "nightmare" child, as Michael put it, threw them for a loop, because none of their reasoned and genuinely loving efforts seemed to repair a situation they thought they should be able to repair. Somewhat typically for two secures, they held the notion: "This wasn't supposed to happen to us. We expect life, at least that part of it we can direct, to turn out pretty darn well." Also typically, however, they're not expending a lot of energy now on feelings of self-recrimination and unproductive questioning. Whether sending Molly to a residential treatment center holds the greatest promise of success is their concern.

Over the course of several sessions, they came at that question from all sides, and in the final analysis, Millie could not answer "yes" in her mind and heart. And once he understood that, Michael was able to put aside his conviction and search with her for another solution, one to which they could both agree. Intensive family counseling, they decided, was a route they hadn't taken and one that might be effective.

Wrestling with those points of difference, and continuing to make yourself known to your partner, helps keep your secure/secure relationship from becoming stagnant, monochromatic, or complacent.

Dig, a Little More, Beneath the Surface

The secure individual is sure of what she knows, and sure, too, of what must be done to get the relationship back on track or to solve a problem. She moves quickly to what she perceives as a necessary action, with a constructive effect. In that rush to act and move forward, however, she is liable to ignore underlying issues that she and her partner would do well to ponder.

Sandra and Bill say they know what to do. "I think sometimes that Bill doesn't fully grasp some of the struggles the kids and I have had in the past," she says. "We were on our own for a number of years, and making this new life hasn't been so easy, even though they really like Bill a lot. And I love him, of course. But he's right to want more of my time. For one thing, I'm pulling back from signing up for some of their school affairs."

"I'm getting the point across to my brother," he says. "He's got to be more respectful of my new family. Helping him move over the past couple of weekends is going to be the end of my major time commitment to him."

This is all to the good. But digging a little deeper would help them understand how each got to those points with the kids and the brother. Some of what Sandra and Bill face now is the need to separate more fully—in emotions, not just time spent—from family members who during unhappy marriages served for each as a displaced source of satisfaction or pleasure. When those good feelings can no longer be obtained from one's partner, finding them elsewhere helps assuage feelings of despair or helplessness. Bill and Sandra, in the process of separating from their former spouses, focused overly on his brother and her kids, respectively; unable to save their marriages, one moved on to save his brother, one moved on to an intimacy with her children that felt safer and more satisfying.

They are working now to correct the imbalance of attentions, setting more limits and keeping the kids and the brother from being too intrusive. And they're capable of accepting the fact that the situation may continue to put a strain on the marriage for a while. But the correction will "take" more profoundly, we point out in our sessions, if they spend a little time quietly contemplating and talking about those deeper currents, which almost inevitably will include some lingering sense of failure attached to their prior marriages. Bill describes that sense in powerful terms: "I've never second-guessed my decision to leave. The situation was intolerable. And with no kids, no big property or money stuff to hassle over, ending it was uncomplicated, in practical terms. But emotionally, I felt like a total loser and washout. It was terribly painful, for a long time."

The fact is, had he never married Sandra, Bill would still have needed to pull back from the rescue mission he was on with his difficult brother. And had she never married Bill, Sandra would still have needed to separate more from her children.

When Jay and Annie started digging a little deeper, they realized that just below the talk of marriage plans lay fear of divorce. These two, being securely attached, took marriage seriously; once in, they weren't planning on getting out (unlike the ambivalent, for example, who may make such a commitment with a more impulsive, what's-the-difference, it-works-or-it-doesn't attitude).

For his part, says Jay: "I think I'm harking back to some pretty lousy role models here. Practically everybody in my family has eventually split up—my *grandparents* got divorced forty years ago, which you'll agree was pretty unusual for that generation and that time." Most painful was his parents' divorce, when he was ten, not long after his father left his mother for another woman. Although Jay's father apparently regretted his actions, Jay's mother refused any attempts at reconciliation and Jay still recalls the mixture of anger and misery he felt over his parents' behaviors.

Annie's parents (although they haven't divorced) separated when she was eighteen: "I had the odd feeling they were just waiting for that birthday of mine, my age of emancipation, when I was deemed old enough to handle it. We all sat down in the living room and they very calmly explained that my dad was going to be moving into an apartment nearby, and it was nobody's fault, they'd grown apart, et cetera, et cetera."

Jay reaches over and gives her hand a squeeze. "Maybe we're tempting fate here by making it legal," he says with a laugh. "Annie and I have it right on the mark right now." She agrees: "I'd say we have it perfect."

Annie selected a telling choice of word. Secure/secure couples expect a kind of perfection. Accustomed to setting and reaching goals, finding satisfaction in accomplishments, and maintaining solid relationships with a variety of people, they have every anticipation of success. Life has to be very good for it to feel good enough.

Their marriage will meet its rocky patches, we tell them, as marriages do. Cracks will appear. They may be disappointed in each other at some point. "The question to ask yourselves," we suggest, "is this one: Must any crack lead to a crash? Is your real concern about marriage based on a conviction that anything short of perfect will lead to a rupture?" They give that one some thought.

The answer, of course, is that the crack need not result in the crash, as long as they are realistic, and can lose the expectation that they'll never be unhappy or upset again. Secures are good at repairing. But the vase that has been broken, cemented back together, and looks fine still contains the crack. Annie and Jay will have to learn to live with the crack, and to decide, if such is the case, that the relationship is sufficiently repaired to be good enough. And then, they must be willing to keep digging below the surface.

In your own relationship, consider whether in your willingness to forgive or make up or just get on with life you may tend to give short shrift to underlying issues. When you feel your partner has a legitimate beef or opinion, you'll make the effort to bring your own actions or attitudes closer to his or her way of thinking. This is well and good, one of the great strengths of secure attachment. But take the time to think: What's wrong here? Do we need to put in more work on this?

When Faced with a Major Decision or a Crisis, Get Some Outside Help

As we've mentioned, we see few secure/secure couples in therapy, simply because they are so good at meeting their problems squarely on their own.

However, when a decision or path about which each may have conflicting feelings arises or there is a major breach of trust by one, this couple can lose some of the strength of their habitual, secure coping mechanisms. Used to the smoothly fluid nature of daily intercourse, the major hit can throw them off the rails, more so than avoidants and ambivalents, who have developed their respective defenses for feelings of anxiety.

Here's the point at which the secure/secure pair can benefit tremendously from counseling. As our three couples demonstrate, they know just what's bothering them, can articulate it clearly, and are ready to start talking. No beating around the bush, no vague expressions of depression or dissatisfaction, but instead, a willingness to work toward reaching some resolution of the matter at hand. They may fight, but the fight will be about the issue and an attempt to find a solution.

In your relationship, try to recognize the point at which your own competence and good sense, and your partner's, could benefit from a helping hand. You are good at expressing your feelings, stating your needs, drawing lines where lines must be drawn, and hearing your partner out. Take those strengths to a professional counselor for some third-party support and advice.

CHAPTER 8

Running To, Running From:

The Secure/Avoidant Couple

HE AND SHE

A very handsome couple sit next to each other on a plush living room couch—we taped this session in their home. He's nursing what looks like a scotch on the rocks, from which she occasionally takes a sip. There's a good deal of laughter and some loving touches, especially from him, as they talk.

HE: Let's start with the first one, paying bills on time.

SHE: I haven't been too great about paying my bills in a timely fashion. There is room for improvement, I know that!

HE: I get annoyed about it, but I think we've worked it out nicely at this point by separating our bills, because fundamentally it doesn't intrude on my life when you make some merchant unhappy. It may bother me on an abstract level, but we've separated our bill paying, and your occasional delinquencies don't intrude on my life, so I accept it. So, paying bills is not a major issue for us. Agreed?

SHE: Agreed. It is not a major issue.

HE: Okay, let's go to number two—"spending too much time at work." Aha, the biggie.

SHE: It's not so much the time you spend working. It's really all the traveling, because I genuinely feel that you could probably accomplish most of what you need to accomplish without flying off to Seattle or San Francisco or wherever all the time.

HE *(looking into the camera, with a smile)*: This one we've been over a few thousand times. *(Back to her.)* At some level you're probably right. But as you know, I have business responsibilities, people depend on me. So for me to conduct my business on the phone would put me in a vulnerable position.

SHE: Okay. You know what I think I'm really saying here? I'd like you around more. I miss you when you're gone.

HE: But what I hear is that you're jealous of my work, that there's some presumption that work is my mistress and I love it more than I love you. *That*, of course, is nonsense. But . . . I don't think we're going to resolve this one. It's sort of the leitmotif of our marriage. And always will be.

SHE: It's gotten better. I've accepted more your being away so much, and I've found more things to do by myself outside of my work.

HE: Well, next question. Now we're getting to the real biggie—"having sex more often."

SHE: What about that is a real biggie?

(He looks at her with a smile, a pause.)

HE: I'm more interested than you are. We know that, right?

SHE: Not exactly.

HE: Well, I don't want to sound sexist here, but I think it's true, the man usually is more interested. The woman usually has the headache, and so on. At the same time, I'm more accepting of this now. I'm older, my sexual desires have decreased. Either I'm older or I'm more mature or both. It doesn't trouble me so much. . . . Anyway, we have a nice time, don't we?

SHE: Yes, I'm very happy with my sex life.

HE: There's our problem . . . you're very happy with it! *(They both laugh.)* But no, sex isn't a huge problem. Okay, next . . . "appreciating each other." Actually, I think this is a very subtle issue. I'm extremely successful in business, I'm kind of an acknowledged statesman in my field. So you meet with a bunch of powerful people and you pull off a fantastic piece of business and you come home, and your wife says, "Take out the garbage." Not quite that maybe, but you get the point. You're not appreciated in your own world, on your own turf.

But I accept it in you. You love me and all, but you don't really appreciate my contributions in other realms.

SHE: I know you're a very successful man and you've done extremely well, and I do appreciate that. I admire you for that. At the same time, it's hard for me to appreciate making money for the sheer joy of making money, and I think the sheer joy of making money is deeply important to you. It's your primary motivator. *(Pause.)* You don't want to talk about this, do you?

HE: Well, the money is good for this. *(He sweeps his arm around the living room.)*

SHE: Of course it is. We enjoy this beautiful home and all mostly because of your efforts. I understand that.

HE: It's not a big issue with me. I guess if I had to rank our problem issues here, spending too much time at work is first—that's been the big, irritating theme of our lives. Okay, do you think I appreciate you?

SHE: Yes, I think you do.

HE: You're right. I do. Let's go on with the list. Next item—"attention to personal appearances." Okay, I was brought up with sisters, appearance is very important to me, and yes, it matters to me a lot how you look. I want you to look great.

SHE: I was brought up the same way. However, it was hugely irritating to me that my mother would never talk about anything except how I looked, how I dressed, why I should dress some other way, my hair. So it's really annoying that I find my husband has the same problem!

I mean, I think I look pretty damn good. Maybe a couple of pounds overweight, but I take care of myself, I buy nice clothes for our events. I even took those boring tap dance lessons!

(After the break, the reconciliation.)

HE: We can talk about anything now? Well, on this appearance thing, on the matter of wanting you to look good . . . I don't defend myself. I feel it's a deep, neurotic element of my being. I can't do much about it.

SHE: But I feel that if I gained ten pounds you might leave me.

HE *(laughing)*: But I really, really love it when you're thin! I love you!

SHE: I don't understand what this deep-seated fear of fat is with you.

HE: It's not fear of fat, it's love of thin! I love thin women who have, you know, nice breasts.

SHE: Well, what would happen if, God forbid, I should lose a breast? Are you out the door then?

(He looks away, says nothing.)

SHE: Suppose I wanted sex a lot more than I do? Suppose I jumped on you every night? But I was ten pounds heavier than I am. Which would you rather have, sex or thin?

HE *(laughing)*: Thin. I'm not a sexist, I'm not a racist, I'm a fattist! *(Looking at the camera again.)* We're both sophisticated individuals here, Mr. Camera Man, and we realize that these matters are not entirely rational.

SHE: Honey, look . . . this concern with appearances, this concern with my weight, I think it makes me feel insecure. I wonder if your head might be turned by some gorgeous, thin thing when you're off on all your business travels!

HE: That's never going to happen.

(The talk drifts off.)

HE: Overall, we're in good shape. I don't want to sound offensive, but this marriage is like an old, comfortable sweater that you can slip right into. It feels good. I enjoy it. I was thinking tonight coming home, what is my idea of a perfect evening? And it's being home with you.

SHE: Well, that's nice.

(Time's up.)

Here's an interesting pair. If you were listening between the lines, you might have heard from him the distinctive voice of the highly socialized avoidant. This is the man (or woman) who comes across to an outsider like Cary Grant (or Deborah Kerr). He's a great guy, a smooth guy, possibly a highly accomplished guy; he knows how to get along in the world, and how to talk with different people. He has manners and the social amenities; he understands the give and take of conversation—now I'm supposed to say something, now you're supposed to say something. Yet, due to his essentially avoidant attachment style, he skirts the issues.

On the videotape, this man is at ease. Although he seems to respond to what his partner is saying, and his conversation is engaging and even affectionate, he ignores her feelings, sticking to the issues he's comfortable with—his ability to make money, his concern for appearances. The charming words come easily—of course I love you more than I love my work, we have a nice time in bed, I can't wait to come home at night and be with you—but there's little emotion behind them.

Like most avoidants, he has only a limited, cautious capacity for intimacy—it makes contact and then it comes apart. We might call this an essentially mental rather than actual state of intimacy; it's one that exists more to meet his needs than those of his partner.

She's basically secure. She keeps bringing up matters of concern to her—I think all that traveling isn't really necessary, I miss you when you're gone, I wouldn't say you're more interested in sex than I am, you're so caught up in how I look that I'm afraid you'll leave me if I gain ten pounds. As she talks about those concerns, she is willing to reveal her own vulnerability to him. And then, trying to get through to him, she comes out with the truly provocative question about how he'd feel if she lost one of those breasts he so adores.

He doesn't respond to her feelings in these matters, however. Explaining his positions in a rather abstract manner, he graciously accepts a measure of blame (okay, I'm neurotic on this score, that's just how it is), rebuffs her protests with a touch of charm (we've been over this one a thousand times before), and deftly avoids the emotional content of her observations. Reaching below the surface makes him uncomfortable.

She wants to draw him closer, but he's not going there. So we can understand why she's a bit underwhelmed by his assertion that his perfect evening is being home with her. Too little, too late, too remote! You say the words, darling, but where is your heart? she might be thinking. She doesn't quite buy his professed affection, because he's essentially unavailable to her, and she knows it.

RAND AND BARBARA

According to Barbara, holiday gatherings and social affairs are some of the times Rand, her husband of ten years, really annoys her. She's a quiet, confident-seeming woman, a full-time mother to the couple's two young children. Rand is a physician.

"Here's an example," she says. "We have a big Christmas party every year, and every year I ask him to clean up the library, which is full of his papers. I remind him several times that we have to use this room. I offer to help him. He does nothing until about an hour before guests arrive, and then we both have to run around like crazy straightening up."

From this and other anecdotes Barbara offers, we gather

that their household is pleasant when Rand can evade involvement in joint concerns. Barbara focuses on all aspects of child-raising and day-to-day life, and Rand focuses on those areas he chooses. When Barbara needs his attention, she presses him and he, reluctantly, complies—for the moment.

Overall, it works well, as do many such secure/avoidant couplings. Most of Barbara's gripes are of the minor, clean-up-your-papers variety. From time to time, however, her avoidant partner has been "not there" for her in ways that hurt. Indeed, she initiated couples therapy when, a year earlier, she became caught up in a low-key flirtation with a divorced father she met when their children exchanged play dates. She accepted two lunch invitations from this man, said nothing about those engagements to Rand, then pulled herself up short. "I thought, 'What am I doing here?' " she says. "I was one step away from starting an affair, I was thinking Rand and I should try a trial separation. I was behaving really out of character, and I knew something was going on with me that I had to figure out."

An astute bit of self-analysis on her part. Barbara's anger at Rand was building to pressure-cooker force. Instead of expressing it to him, an exercise she had experienced over time as futile and frustrating, she began to act out her feelings—toying with that flirtation, entertaining the notion of a separation. With her essentially secure way of trying to get more of what she needed from her husband not working too well, she was provoked into some of those more ambivalent behaviors. But they were "out of character," she knew.

After a few solo sessions with the counselor, Barbara persuaded her husband to join her. For his part, although he has made some progress, Rand still wishes his wife realized how much he loves her, and appears totally baffled that she sometimes seems not to know that.

TONI AND CHRIS

They met at an AA meeting—"a great place to hook up with cute guys who've learned a few things about life," says Toni with a laugh. They're both professional chefs on the staffs of two separate high-end restaurants, and have a dream of someday opening their own place. "What cooks do when they go off duty," she continues more seriously, "is go out to another restaurant and sit around drinking wine and talking food." Each was both startled and excited, at that first meeting four years ago, to find another soul with the same profession, the same dream, and the same determination that it was enough with the wine.

Both in their mid-thirties and divorced, they have been living together for three years. Chris is a big man with a bushy beard; Toni is a big woman with a fresh-faced, well-scrubbed, no-nonsense look to her. Her conversation is as straightforward as her looks. "Our sex life is fairly tame," she says. "On second thought, make that fairly lousy."

Chris, says Toni, had become over the past year perfectly content with sex once a month or less, and he rebuffs her advances. Toni, says Chris, doesn't pay attention to his cues—he's willing to be a little more active but she doesn't seem to pick up on his moods. Several months earlier Toni had, once again, aired her dissatisfaction with their sex life, and suggested her boyfriend go for a physical checkup. Toni continues: "Chris resisted that idea. Instead, he asked me how much sex was a 'normal' amount. I thought that was kind of an odd question, but I said I guessed about three times a week sounded nice to me. He said, 'Fine, we'll try for that.' "

Chris, in his avoidant wish to cut off any deeper discussion and escape further conflict, tried to solve the problem by agreeing to perform on a schedule. The problem, it comes as no surprise, was not solved; Chris soon reverted to his infrequent desire for sex. That was the point at which Toni insisted he pursue the idea of a medical checkup to see if any physical explanation for his low sex drive existed and, if his doctor thought it a good idea, join her in some couples counseling.

"Chris is the best thing that's happened in my personal life in a long time," she says. "We're a great pair in many ways. But I do think that when things are not working in bed, it's probably an indication of something else that's off in the relationship."

Chris has some trouble agreeing with this assessment—"We do have a great relationship," he says, "it's just this one area"—but he's sufficiently committed to Toni to have agreed to try to talk out the situation.

JACKIE AND RUSSELL

Jackie, fifty-six, has been married for twenty-five years to a man who she says "overall, has more qualities on the plus side than the minus side."

The marriage has been a bumpy ride. Through all those years, the major problem has been Russell's inability to maintain a steady job and provide an adequate income for his family. A voracious reader and lover of books, he's held a series of positions in the publishing business, each one, says Jackie, "starting out with a bang and fizzling out within the space of two or three years." One such fizzle she learned about only a week after the fact, when she happened to spot her newly unemployed mate sitting in the local library reading in mid-afternoon. He hadn't told her he was again on the street, a classic demonstration of avoidant attachment.

She thinks—she *knows*, she says—a large part of the difficulty has been "Russ's failure to present himself forcefully, to work well with other people in an industry where you're supposed to have ideas and convictions." Besides, she says, her husband is "pathologically disorganized, doesn't follow through on things. You can never assume that something he says he's going to do will actually get done. This has been a maddening issue in our private life, so I'm assuming it's also been a factor in why his career turned out the way it did, or why it didn't turn out at all."

But in a turn for the better, Russell, who's five years older than Jackie, has recently developed his own small business hand-printing and binding special editions of books, collections of poetry and folk tales that he sells at craft shows and through specialty shops. "He's happy as a clam," she says. "This is perfect for him. He shares a piece of an artist's studio downtown, he works completely on his own, he doesn't have to answer to anybody." His income from this enterprise, however, covers the cost of his supplies and not a whole lot else.

So, we ask, how about those pluses over the years? Jackie pauses. "I was about to say he's been a really good father to our two girls," she says, "but that's not quite accurate. A good father, to my way of thinking, takes care of business first—the nuts-and-bolts part of parenthood, so to speak. Which is what my father did. You pay attention to the tedious, stressful stuff, like getting the bills paid and the taxes done and the kids to the doctor. That's been left to me. What Russ has been is a delightful, playful, charming father to our kids, and I do value that enormously because they've turned out so beautifully well—funny, bright, generous young adults. Especially when they were little, he was like the Pied Piper with them and their friends. Kids loved him."

Jackie has enjoyed Russell's playful nature herself, some of the time. "Russ always seemed like a bit of a cockeyed optimist, like that 'What, me worry?' character." Over time, however, she perceived that demeanor as one more of denial than of optimism: "He didn't worry enough about things that needed to be worried about, so I ended up worrying more."

She and her partner, she thinks, are at a crossroads now. With their daughters grown and living their own lives, and with her own long-term job as executive assistant to a university dean still secure and the money pressures eased, Jackie is reassessing the picture. "Well, obviously, we're not getting younger," she says. "This is the time we should start exploring some options for the future, like do we at some point sell the house and perhaps move to a less expensive part of the country?" But she is tired of being the worrier, "the responsible one."

For a while, too, she indulged in some "is this all there is?" soul searching, thinking that maybe she'd like to kick up her heels a little, take off on her own for a while. She decided she didn't, not really, but needed to get Russell and herself on a better track. She has come to talk things out on her own for several sessions, and Russell says he'll join her later.

It's not by accident that, as you may have noticed, our couple fits here all involve the secure woman attached to the avoidant man. Certainly, the vice-versa match occurs, but in counseling this is a combination we see often—the competent, articulate, emotionally sturdy wife or girlfriend and the unemotional, unavailable husband or boyfriend.

In the early stages of a love affair, the avoidant man might seem an appealingly, sexily remote challenge to the secure partner, a guy ripe to be opened up by the right woman. Indeed, that's a scenario that has provided the plot line of a great mush of romance fiction. Think of Robert Kincaid, the self-described "one of the last cowboys" of *The Bridges of Madison County*. Starting out, rolling down Route 2 toward Iowa in his beat-up truck, Robert is a man "as alone as it's possible to be," a man who "knew scarcely anyone well, nor they him." A few cameras, a carton of Camels, and a Swiss Army knife are about all he needs, although he thinks having a dog would be nice. Then he meets Francesca Johnson, a woman with the insight to acknowledge the limitations and responsibilities of her life and the courage to follow her heart, and in the blink of an eye Robert is proclaiming himself a changed man. "This is why I'm here on this planet," he tells her, ". . . to love you." He recites poetry. He empathetically accepts those responsibilities that will keep Francesca in her marriage. He even cries.

Robert and Francesca have less than a week together, so the quintessential fantasy of the distant man transformed by love never gets put to the test of time. In the real world, it's a transformation unlikely to happen in the first place. And in the long run, the secure may feel disillusioned eventually, for there will always be a limit to what she gets back from her partner. Nevertheless, such couple fits often give off a comfortable atmosphere of accommodation. Living with an avoidant partner can be pleasurable for the independent-minded secure. She enjoys doing her own thing and has her own thing to do, as all the women in our examples reveal. Barbara, although she has no outside job, is deeply satisfied with her decision to raise the kids and run the family's social life. She, securely, feels in no way depleted or put upon, and she, like our other women, has nourishing friendships, hobbies, and interests. The secure's partner, in his ongoing effort not to connect, won't interfere with any of this.

Often that avoidant man is professionally at the top of his game; that's where he sees his success, as a good businessman or an admired doctor, just as he considers being that kind of success as doing all he needs to do for his family. If the avoidant is a person of accomplishment, as were some of our men, the secure also finds much to admire there. A lot of the time, that admiration compensates for whatever disappointments she may feel about his emotional unavailability or lack of involvement. Even Jackie (who, she says, "long ago came to terms with the reality that I was going to be the main provider for this family") sees the broad picture of her marriage and her husband. She speaks of the respect she has for his dedication to his craft and feels he's played a major role in the blossoming of their children—that together, she as "the nuts-and-bolts" worrier, and he as "the Pied Piper," balanced each other and did a good job as parents.

It's a good couple fit for the avoidant, too, who relies on his partner to keep things running smoothly or to allow him to pursue his own priorities and schedules.

However, on the negative side of the ledger, a child's difficulties, illness, sudden family troubles, sex problems, or any other major issue may well find this pair unaccustomed to working as a real team, with potentially damaging effects.

And then, the real danger: For the secure partner, the accumulation over time of feelings of distance, loneliness, lack of connection, even rejection, may somewhere down the line lead to that "is this all there is?" questioning. She may drift away, as Barbara did for a time, or find a lover; she hopes for another chance at a genuinely intimate relationship. Indeed, the slow drift that might take place in this couple fit can also prompt the avoidant partner to search for romance outside the relationship. If feeling pushed to participate and perform, he may turn to an affair out of anger and a need to prove to himself that he really is capable of involvement.

TOWARD A MORE COMFORTABLE COUPLE FIT

FOR THE SECURE

Drag Your Partner In on the "Small Stuff"

Jackie describes the frustration she has so often felt when trying to get her husband's attention: "In the old days, sometimes I'd get so mad that I'd go over and snap off the TV while he was watching. Once I threw out a pile of his antiquarian magazines because I'd been asking him for weeks to file them away somewhere." She used to, she says now with a laugh, "follow him around the house like a prosecuting attorney to continue a discussion he was determined not to have."

Those tactics sometimes spurred Russell into temporary compliance with a one-time request, although they did nothing to change his powerful need to avoid true engagement with his partner. Over time, Jackie started taking care of more and more on her own, without attempting to drag Russell in. "I was good at being the bookkeeper, as I've thought of it," she says, "and it just took less out of me to handle things myself than to go through an argument or an explanation of what needed to be done." She realizes now that this behavior hasn't served either of them well in the long run: "I effectively cut Russ off from a lot that he should have been in on, even if I was the one who had to get him there. If we stick it out—and really I do want the marriage to go on—we have to pull together more, because there are some big decisions coming up that we have to make." Over the last year or so, she says, she has been working at finding some middle ground "between being the shrew and hassling him, which doesn't work, and cutting him off, which isn't so great either."

If obtaining your partner's cooperation or attention is an ongoing struggle, perhaps you have found it's emotionally less taxing to leave him out of much of the daily nitty-gritty. It's understandable, but not the best way to go.

Do keep making the effort to get him to sit up and take notice, because the "small stuff" has a cumulative, negative effect. Let's say, for example, your partner does a weekly supermarket run and prides himself (in his typically avoidant way) on shopping the sales and finding the bargains. And one of his bargains has been rolls of inexpensive paper towels imprinted with blue teddy bears. And you detest the sight of those bears in your sleekly modern kitchen, but say nothing because teddy bears on paper towels, you decide, are unimportant.

Your annoyance, however, building from this and a dozen other similarly "unimportant" actions, *is* worth paying attention to. These seemingly minor behaviors on your partner's part are symptomatic of an attachment style that you will often find difficult to live with. Perhaps you really do need to tell him you want only plain white heavy-duty Bounty because you can't stand the blue teddy bears in your kitchen, and he can buy the Bounty or you will.

For another thing, sooner or later you may have to make some of those big decisions Jackie mentions, and pull together more.

So get in the habit of talking to your avoidant mate about mini-crises, such as your teenager's plan to drop band or your mother's determination to move to a new apartment. Although you typically deal with these things on your own, say, "This is important to me. I need you to pay attention to this." You really *can* encourage a greater degree of involvement, although not without effort.

Press for Action, Not Analysis

In the He/She dialogue that opens this chapter, the wife voices her opinion that her husband may not really need to do all that traveling for his work. She's probably got that right. We've found that many an avoidant tends to travel on business a lot, get out of town, keep busy, keep moving, keep avoiding. But he's not about to speculate on any deeper motives for his actions. He will not open up. She then expresses her discontent in more personal terms. "I'd like you around more," she says. "I miss you when you're gone." He explains her feelings as a problem of jealousy, then wraps up the discussion by decreeing that they will never get this one solved.

If her unhappiness over his traveling really is "the biggie," the "leitmotif" of their relationship, they would do well to keep trying to solve it. She might obtain more of what she wants by sticking to expressed wishes for particular actions— I really want us to go together to that concert next Friday, so unless it's a life-or-death business emergency, please be here. And then she must not allow him to distract them both with intellectualized comments on the nature of his work.

Toni was on the mark when she concluded that the difficulties she and Chris were having over too much/too little sex probably had some connection to relationship issues beyond the bedroom. And she did press for appropriate action—ruling out the possibility of a physical reason for what's going on and then seeing what else might be getting in the way.

Over the course of a few talks, Chris and Toni revealed that his family—specifically, his mother's hold on her only son—might be one of those issues. Toni described a recent argument. His parents expect Toni and Chris to return to the old homestead in Connecticut for a family get-together this upcoming Christmas, as they had the previous two years.

The two of them had already discussed this expected invitation—"more like being summoned to a command performance," Toni says—and decided that since they'd been working extraordinarily long hours and the get-together would be anything but relaxing, they would decline, stay home, and take in a couple of movies. Instead, when Mom started turning the screws, Chris put her off over the phone with a lot of hemming and hawing, and then when he could dodge her no longer said Toni might have to work over the holiday.

Toni was mad. "Your family is like a bunch of bananas, Chris," she says to him now. "They can only move together, lockstep. You're thirty-five years old. Time to separate from the bunch. Be yourself. Stop hiding behind me. And stop worrying so much about being the nice guy and not making your mother mad."

Chris thinks maybe they should work out some compromise, such as going up later and coming back earlier, and he knows, he says, that Toni doesn't like those people very much. To which Toni replies: "This isn't about compromise, this is about you growing up. This is about you being a bad son if you say what you want and get your own life. And true, I don't much like them, but admit it, *you* don't like those people much either. If you all love each other so much, how come none of you know that yet? How come everybody walks on tiptoes?"

Chris, actually, is aware of all this already. Now he talks about other occasions, when one or the other of his sisters was in the doghouse with his parents for not toeing the line, for not showing enough concern for the family, or for being too independent. "They *are* a bunch of bananas," he says.

Chris learned at an early age that the price for insisting on his own wishes resulted in his parents', especially his mom's, disapproval and emotional withdrawal. While he's bold to the point of being a great risk taker on the job, the stakes are still too high for Chris to stand up to his parents. Within his avoidant attachment pattern, issues of separation and abandonment provoke deep anxieties.

Toni has a pretty keen understanding of what happens in her boyfriend's interactions with his family. She gets frustrated with the situation, and articulates it clearly and directly, with a minimum of attack. Chris is starting to feel stronger, in no small part because he has a partner who is responsive to him in an affectionate, clear, and honest manner. She's good at expressing her feelings; he's getting better at not avoiding his. However, it will help neither of them if Toni continues to express Chris's feelings for him.

She sees this: "I have a tendency, I know, to tell him what he feels, because he simply won't acknowledge so much that goes on." Pull back for a moment, we suggest, and consider the immediate desired result—to skip that family get-together—and how it might best be achieved.

"Chris has good talking skills," Toni says suddenly, with a laugh. "He can state his thoughts very clearly in his work and when we're out with friends. He should use his talking skills to simply tell his folks we won't be there."

This is a good idea, and a useful press for action on her part. Toni uses her observations of her boyfriend's capacities constructively, supports his strengths, and has a better chance of getting her desired result than if she nags him to ponder his need to "grow up."

Another example: Barbara has regular flare-ups of pique because Rand's long hours mean the family doesn't see much of him. Her tendency at those times has been to voice her concerns, to little effect. She's learning instead to tell him, specifically, what she needs him to do, and that is proving more successful, most of the time. Like all avoidants, Rand is better able to change his behavior in response to a request for action ("I think it would be great if you made time to walk Alex to school once or twice a week") than to an emotional complaint or even perfectly legitimate observation ("I'm upset because the kids hardly get to spend any time with you at all, and I think they miss that").

A little analysis probably goes a long way with your avoidant partner. Push the underlying emotional issues, talk about feelings or motives and you may run into a brick wall. But you can get a lot more of what you want or need simply by focusing on actions and going light on the analysis.

Moreover, at a time of crisis, you may benefit from your partner's ability to act and snap you out of what may have become an emotionally wrought overanalysis of the problem at hand. Secures tend to jump into a big issue with all four feet; they engage. For example, if somebody needs a heart operation, they will be on the phone all day with every surgeon in the country and online all night downloading the latest research. They can overengage and overreact.

When several years ago it became apparent that their younger child had learning difficulties, for example, Barbara left no stone unturned in her efforts to find the cause and the solution, putting her son through a battery of tests and putting *herself* through more tests to search for genetic influences. "She became a little crazed over the whole thing," Rand says as they talk over that time in one of our sessions. "Finally it was decided that Sam has dyslexia and other information-processing difficulties, and would benefit from tutoring, but Barbara kept racing around for further opinions and recommendations. Then she started working with Sam at home and making *him* a little crazy too."

Barbara, in retrospect, agrees she became "overinvested." Although she still claims that Rand was on the underinvested side, she acknowledges that his more coolly unemotional approach helped them reach a sound decision. "I'd interviewed about four tutors and finally Rand said this was no good, we had to settle on a plan. He talked to this woman, he talked to Sam's teacher, we got a program started. The report from school was good, and Rand told me it was really time for me to back off," she says. "And he was right."

Like many avoidants, Rand is a man who likes to be "the fixer." He steps in and resolves a problem (but might, perhaps, step right out again). This can be an enormously useful trait at times for his secure partner.

Don't Back Your Partner into a Corner (At Least, Not Too Often)

In our counseling sessions, the avoidant mate of a secure partner will often say, "She's always pushing my buttons." To which we think, but usually do not say, "How about you changing your buttons?" Changing his buttons is no easy task for the easily wounded avoidant. While he is capable of complying with a specific request for action, as we have noted, it is often with a certain amount of anxiety or feeling put upon. If he starts feeling backed into a corner, the only way he can come out of it is by fighting, which is a useful fact for you to understand.

Here's an example: Barbara worries that her children are growing up with essentially minimum contact with one of their parents, and that will be to everyone's misfortune in the long run. It's a legitimate concern, but although she's achieved some of those small, walk-Alex-to-school-today compliances from him, Barbara has made a few bad calls in her continued effort to press for his engagement.

"Last month," she recalls, "it was open school night at the kids' school, and I told Rand I thought he ought to be there with me. He said he had to work and I was annoyed. Let him stay up until three to get his work done, I thought, but he should haul himself over to this parent thing. So I just signed up that he would be there and I told the kids he was going."

Rand did attend that school function, simultaneously in a foul mood and on his best "official" behavior. "She knew I had a lot going on at work," he says, "and basically she just embarrassed me or shamed me into going. It was like black-mailing me with my children." The fallout was not pretty—"several days of his quiet seething, being sarcastic, acting in slightly snotty little ways," she says. This was Rand's mode of coming out fighting.

Barbara thinks now she should have simply supported him. She should have explained to the children that he probably wouldn't be able to make visiting night and allowed him to save face. Whether he was there or not wasn't such a big deal with the kids, she acknowledges. However, in the toss-up she chose the path that backed him into a corner and made life unpleasant for a while.

Barbara could trace the direct arc from her school-night actions and his "sarcastic" behavior later. The arc may not always be so clear in your couple fit. A troublesome aspect of life with an avoidant partner reflects the fact that you don't always know what will set him off. Press his button at nine A.M. Monday morning and the bomb may not go off until Saturday afternoon. It may not be a bomb at all, but passive-aggressive fighting back or some of that "slightly snotty" attitude.

For the sake of a more comfortable couple fit, try not to back your partner into a corner. Never having learned a good way to handle conflict, the avoidant is usually contained, but, as we noted in our profile, often at a price of increasing fury. When he explodes, the eruption can be destructive. What will get him angry is what he perceives as an insensitivity to his feelings, a slight that at some deep level stirs up the avoidant's ancient fears of abandonment: "If my partner knows not or cares little for what I feel, she's left me," is how we might state (or somewhat overstate) the emotion.

Don't Resent Having to Be the Initiator

Toni started making a concerted effort to put some oomph back in the sex life that had been dying on the vine. She asked Chris to talk to her about those cues he thought she always missed, and she figured out how she might express her own "advances" in ways that were more comfortable to him. She explains that she has "been arranging for us to get a little change of scenery once in a while." They spent two days pretending they were honeymooning at a nice hotel, another couple of days camping. "It's amazing how sexy zipping yourselves into a double sleeping bag can be," she says, and Chris gives out a little chuckle.

However, she adds: "It kind of pisses me off that I'm doing all the work here." "What work?" we ask. "Starting the talks, checking out the hotel, getting the campground information, all that," she says. "Has all that work been paying off?" She acknowledges that it has; they are sexually enjoying each other better and more often. So, we ask: "If you're accomplishing some of what you hoped to accomplish, does it matter whether you or Chris was the one who picked up the phone and made the hotel reservation or ordered the sleeping bag?" She guesses that it doesn't.

This is an adjustment Toni may have to make, a fact she must accept and remind herself of over time, if she is to find greater comfort in her couple fit: She will probably always be the one who recharges the relationship as needed. As long as he responds, as long as it "works," she must tell herself that that is the objective and that's enough. Giving up the annoyance and "pissed" feeling may be difficult for her, though—because it's not so much the excess of work on her part as the lack of drive on her partner's part that's bothering her. She will probably never receive from Chris all of what she would like in terms of passion and drive, but clearly, as he's demonstrated, she can receive more of what she needs.

For Jackie, being the initiator has meant "making lists for Russell," she says. Over the years she has blown up on occasion, complaining to her partner about his inability or unwillingness to recognize matters that need attention. "It's not simply that he doesn't *do* the thing, he doesn't even see that it needs doing." Russell usually has responded to one of those blowups by saying, "Tell me what you want me to do and I'll take care of it." She would then draw up a list of the six or eight items on the current agenda—replace the doorknob in the bathroom, call for mortgage refinancing forms—all the while fuming silently. It's that "tell me what *you want* me to do" that riles her, she says, "as if the defective doorknob or whatever has nothing to do with him but is just some notion I have that he'll carry out as a favor."

Certainly, Jackie has a legitimate beef, but holding on to the beef simply serves to keep her angry. The fact is, we suggest, she may never get the bottom-line satisfaction she's after, which is that her partner will realize a need to act in a more mature and responsible manner. If she can expect and accept instead a next-to-the-bottom-line achievement— the doorknob will get replaced and that's one thing she won't have to do—she is likely to find a much greater measure of internal peace. As they enter a new phase of life, when big decisions such as selling the house, relocating, or securing an investment income will have to be addressed, Jackie knows she'll be making a lot of those lists. At least, we point out, her avoidant partner is likely to comply with her requests; were she married to an ambivalent, she would more probably be faced with a "tell me what you want me to do so I won't do it" attitude.

As you go about accepting the reality of your own secure/avoidant couple fit, ask yourself: What's the difference who initiates what? In the grand scheme of things, it doesn't really matter a lot if you, and never your partner, are the one who says, "Gee, why don't we go out for dinner tonight?" or "Let's get away for a weekend, just the two of us." You may have to be the initiator in all areas of your relationship, the one who starts a conversation about a new book, or throws out suggestions about getting together with friends, or talks about moving to a bigger apartment. It may be frustrating, but does it make a difference?

Here's what *does* make a difference: Is a concern that needs addressing being addressed or not? Is a good idea being acted on or not?

We will digress a bit here and say that resentment over having to be the one who starts the ball rolling is a huge issue with many pairs we see in counseling, even the secure/secure couples. It's a huge issue because the initiator perceives his or her partner's inaction as a lack of love, thinking, "If you really cared about me and our relationship, *you'd* suggest we go out to dinner tonight." For the perpetual initiator, resentment brews out of that "proof" of love, rather than annoyance at having to do all the work, although the latter is the more readily identifiable issue. In therapy, we try to take this one off the table right away. Being the one who always moves things forward may be irksome, but really, it's a matter of little importance.

Even in the minor bits of business of your joint life, perhaps you are usually the actor and your partner is the reactor. He never notices that the lamp needs rewiring or the plane reservations must be changed. Then, even if he takes care of the lamp or the reservations, you think it doesn't count because you told him what to do. Overcome these feelings, or at least work at keeping them in perspective.

Don't Hero-Worship

The secure partner in many secure/avoidant couples we have counseled is quick to point out the excellent qualities possessed by his or her mate.

While articulate and specific about their complaints, Barbara and Toni, for example, are equally eager to praise their partners. Rand is a brilliant doctor who's dedicated to helping humanity; Chris is a creative genius and rising star of the restaurant business. Even Jackie, whose unhappiness with her partner once reached a serious degree, decided ultimately the good outweighed the bad.

Several years ago, Jackie considered ending the marriage. Russell's lack of career and financial success and his unwillingness to involve her in those aspects of his life were deeply disappointing to her. "I felt at the time," she says, "that if he had only been able to talk to me about these matters, which would have had to involve talking about his feelings of inadequacy—and I know he did feel inadequate—things would have been better. He needed to change. *I* needed him to change, not in the sense of making big money, but to change his style of relating to me, so we could work out these problems together."

Being securely attached, Jackie was accustomed to having her needs met. Unwilling to tolerate consistent disappointment, Jackie was on the point of pulling out—just when her husband established his own business and clearly restored a measure of self-esteem, and just when their children became more independent. And then as Russell, with her encouragement, did slowly start inching toward a greater degree of openness, Jackie discovered that her reservoir of love and good feelings toward him carried the day. Although he's still often maddeningly uninvolved, she speaks fondly of Russell as "the master craftsman" and "the Pied Piper."

Like Barbara, Toni, and Jackie, the secure tends to always find the separate identity and strength in the other to respect and acknowledge with approval, which is a powerful factor in motivating each to stay with his or her partner and work at making the fit more comfortable. Carried to an extreme, however, that acceptance and praise can be a kind of hero worship that prompts the secure to turn too many blind eyes.

Possibly your partner inspires your admiration, because she's controlled, stoic, and strong. And as a secure, you naturally remember and value her good qualities, which is fine. Do not, however, let your tendency to focus on the positive become the sustaining feature of your relationship, and perhaps the means by which you ignore many of your unmet needs.

FOR THE AVOIDANT

As you read our suggestions and then, ideally, act on them, don't downplay their importance or your achievement because the suggestions come from us. Here is a kind of exchange we often run across in counseling sessions that include one avoidant partner: "How about you two getting away from the household for a while, have a weekend in the country, hire a babysitter and go out dancing?" we say. "Well, we could do that, but it won't mean much, will it, because you're telling us to do it," says our avoidant.

It will mean much, or at least has a chance to, regardless of who came up with the idea. Making excuses, not taking the "homework" seriously, and minimizing the importance of attempting small changes, all reflect your natural resistance to alter the couple fit. Try to get over it.

When Angry, Annoyed, or in Conflict with Your Partner, Say So

This won't be easy for you, because touching base with those uncomfortable feelings, much less talking about them, is awfully unpleasant. Besides, your secure partner can comfortably and clearly express what she wants or thinks should happen. Your tendency is to go along, since she seems so sure—and anyway, what's the point, you think, in stirring things up? When you are inclined to accommodate your partner's wishes, ask yourself if you really do share her opinion—or if you're only acting as if you do in order to avoid a confrontation or to be left alone.

Here's an even tougher question to ask yourself: Can the behaviors that get your partner riled be attributed to your passive-aggressive need to not do what she wants you to do?

Barbara points out to Rand, and he cannot disagree, that on many occasions he has willfully "forgotten" an appointment, an agreement, or a chore because it didn't suit him to remember it. "For example, we had concert tickets recently, I told him about it, he wrote down the date in his calendar, I reminded him that morning even," she says, "and then he got home late and looked surprised to see me waiting there dressed up and fuming." She would have much preferred, she says, if he had simply told her at the start that he really would rather not go to the concert and then perhaps she could have invited her friend instead: "This would be no huge blow to me and, obviously, I'd end up a whole lot less angry than I did."

That, of course, is difficult for him; it is far easier to avoid the unwanted action by not taking it.

A rather complex bit of business is going on here. The avoidant is not simply contrary; he fears a loss of autonomy if he does what his partner wants. It's a fear of being trapped, which paradoxically rises from a fear of his own wish to merge. He wants to get closer, but getting closer and complying with his partner's wishes means he loses his independence. So he keeps his distance.

Rand or any avoidant need not spend a lot of time pondering those dynamics. He just needs to practice speaking out more often about what he wants and doesn't want, what's made him angry and why. His secure partner can give him a boost in this effort by encouraging him to recognize the times he is feeling one thing but saying another, or not saying much of anything.

Barbara picks up on this idea right off the bat and reminds her partner of this recent incident. "After that dinner party last month, when I put your grandmother's dessert plates in the dishwasher, you came in the kitchen when I was unloading the washer and one of the plates had been chipped. You picked it up and said, 'Look at this' and walked out, disapproval radiating from your pores! I know that's a valuable set of china and it has a big family connotation. I also know it wasn't very bright of me to put them through the dishwasher. Why couldn't you just say you were upset and that this china should be handled very carefully?" Rand gets the idea too.

Give Your Partner Signs and Signals of Appreciation

A "delicious treat" throughout the many years of her marriage, says Jackie, has been her husband's repeated, small demonstrations of the love and affection he does have for her: "In some of those big ways—the security and reassurance of having a steady job, of taking care of a lot of family matters—he wasn't able to give to me. I really don't know why. Sometimes I think he never found the right fit for his own life." She laughs. "He's a guy who probably should have been a monk in a medieval monastery, illuminating manuscripts."

She guesses that he suspects she's "felt gypped in this marriage at times." And he's made the effort to show her he appreciates her, in ways he can. He's brought her flowers, made hand-painted cards for her birthdays and their anniversaries, and even organized the kids for a mom's-day-in-bed breakfast.

Not all avoidant partners put thought into the signs and signals of appreciation. If you don't, you should.

Things—flowers and little gifts—are good. Hugs, kisses, and comments that show you like something she's done are also good. Use these ways to demonstrate your love, and relieve a little of that pressure to verbalize your feelings.

Try, at Odd Moments, to Define Your Partner's Mood

A secure or ambivalent, if asked to guess what a partner might be thinking or feeling at any particular time, usually will be not far off the mark. Toni, for example, says, "I just know by the way Chris shuts the door when he gets in at night and by the level of his eyelids that he is annoyed about something that happened at work. It always turns out I'm right, too." The secure very likely will be empathetic then, and feel bad that the other is upset or glad that he's happy. The ambivalent, stirred up by all that awareness of her partner's emotions, may pick a mini-fight about something. She is resisting her feelings and pushing her partner to feel any other way than the way he does at the moment. In either case, a response takes place, because secures and ambivalents are able to attain a sufficient closeness to cue in to what is going on in the partner's head.

As an avoidant, however, you probably have a tougher time picking up prevailing emotional currents. Try to improve your skills in this regard, for the sake of promoting a closer couple fit.

As an exercise in tuning in, look at your partner and try to guess what is on her mind: "She looks distracted and a bit hyper, which I would guess has to do with that unsatisfactory phone conversation she had yesterday with her sister and with anticipation of the lunch she'll have today with her boss." Then, ask her and find out whether you are right.

Become Aware of Your Inclination to Hear Suggestions As Criticisms

Toni became concerned at one point that her boyfriend wasn't getting enough fun out of life. "Chris is a workaholic," she says. "Seventy percent of him is in the restaurant, the other thirty percent is with me. He should do something just for himself, just for the enjoyment of it. I've been telling him he ought to get back to tennis. He played in college and he was great at it." So far, Chris has made no move toward the courts. Maybe he will get around to that, he says.

"Getting around to it" will probably not happen, for a couple of reasons. First, Chris hears his partner's "Why don't you go out and play some tennis?" as a criticism. Perhaps she believes that he's not doing enough, he's not interesting enough, he's getting fat, she wants him out of her hair. Second, it's been ingrained in him that he's not *supposed* to do something just for himself, just for the enjoyment of it.

Toni's suggestion—and it sounds like a loving and sensible one—would have a better chance of taking hold if she presented it slightly differently: "Why don't we play a little tennis next Saturday? You can give me some pointers." Luring him thusly into this joint outing might work for two reasons. First, they'll do it together and her partner can borrow from her some of the secure's ability to sink into the moment and enjoy the activity. Second, Chris can accede more easily to the tennis idea since it is a thing he's doing for his partner, not himself, and that makes his avoidant's heart glad. If all goes well, Toni can then say, "Gee, you seemed to have a great time today," which might start Chris reflecting on the fact that he really does like playing tennis.

And if all goes well in the long run, he might gradually stop hearing his partner's suggestions as criticisms. This is a good lesson for any avoidant to learn.

Say to Yourself Regularly, "My Partner Is a True Friend"

When he pushes, his aim is to create a helpful alliance, not to submerge, control, or frustrate you.

The hope, and the strong possibility, in the secure/avoidant couple fit is that the love relationship is mature enough, or will mature sufficiently over time, for each partner to grow in degrees of accommodation. The secure has the capacity to accept a lot of avoidant behavior, and doesn't always need the partner to change emotionally. This is an enormous plus for this pair, because the avoidant will probably always be limited in how far she can expand her own capacity for handling emotions.

CHAPTER 9

The Owl and the Hummingbird:
The Secure/Ambivalent Couple

HE AND SHE

THIS mid-thirtyish couple looked from the start ready to have a little fun with their assignment. Throughout their ten minutes of talk, a teasing, provocative air prevailed. She thought they ought to start off with "disciplining the children."

SHE: I've said this before—you yell at the kids too much. I think you're banking on an idea that you're special in some way, you're different, and your behavior toward them isn't going to affect them. And I say it's going to backfire. The kids are genuinely fearful of you. You're scary sometimes! I get scared! Also, they're getting used to yelling as a way to respond to things—they're learning that this is how a person handles differences.

HE: That's true that I'm a shouter. But, number one, I

can't control the way I am. You think I yell because I have some child-raising theory about how to get through to kids? You're wrong. The way I deal with the kids is just how I was raised—it's my instinctive reaction. I try to control my temper. I'm not always successful, but you'd see how it would be if I didn't try to control it. A whole lot worse, trust me. Very often I lose it, I know that, but it's difficult to change the way I am.

SHE: Then get some therapy and figure out how to deal with it better. Because I really worry that we're going to produce these horrible children who grow up yelling.

HE *(with a smile)*: It's interesting you picked this topic, isn't it? Here's the one you know you can take the moral high ground on. You're right, I'm wrong.

(She seems to make a conscious decision to switch gears at this point, and takes another look at the list.)

SHE: What about this, "accepting praise"?

HE: I'd say you have a serious problem accepting praise. A serious emotional problem being able to accept praise for the things you do well.

SHE *(laughing)*: Should I respond to that?

HE: Of course you should respond. What, are you worried about seeming domineering here? The reality is, you are indeed the dominant party! The dominatrix!

SHE: Well, I think I need to get more praise or maybe I do need to respond better to praise I get . . . but you're right, I always think I should be doing a lot of things a lot better than I do, and that's a problem I have.

HE: This is hardly surprising, of course, considering that mother of yours.

SHE: But I'd say you have a problem too. Like, if I have to work late a couple of nights in a row, you go crazy because I'm not paying attention to you.

HE: That's a reality, those are my needs.

SHE: You think I don't pay attention to you ninety percent of the time?

HE: Not enough. What difference does it make if you think it's ninety percent and that's enough? For me, it's not enough. These are my needs.

SHE: Admit it, you'd like one hundred percent of my attention.

HE: No, wrong, absolutely wrong.

SHE: You know, you don't pay a lot of attention to me. You never ask me how my day was, for instance. You like it when the kids say, "What did you do today, Daddy?" I don't hear that kind of attention from you.

HE: Hey, I call you at your office a couple of times a day. What other husband does that? Like today, in fact, I called you four times—once after you'd already left.

(Another retreat, back to the list. They talk over a few more items and agree, they both say: No major problems, no big differences or difficulties, except for that matter of how to handle the kids.)

HE *(with a laugh)*: How about being dull? Could we talk about your dullness? Like maybe some new meals once in a while? We might be able to get a little more creative meals on the table?

SHE *(giggling)*: Yeah, and maybe you could get some of those meals on the table from time to time?

HE: My answers for meals and sex are the same—a little more creativity.

(She returns to the issue of her concern for the kids, that maybe they're developing an aggressive streak, and starts describing an argument she had that day with their son.)

HE: No, we're not talking about your fight with Owen. We're supposed to be talking about our feelings here. I feel you do a fine job with the kids, and it's too bad you feel you're inadequate.

SHE: That's not really the point I'm making. I think that with them you're barking orders a lot of the time. They're getting a sense that that's the way to deal with issues, as I said. Well, is there anything we're going to do about this? I think part of this exercise is that we're supposed to try to resolve the issue, not just talk about feelings.

HE: See, that's the problem . . . you impose the rules. You're always imposing the rules.

(When the therapist comes in to conclude their ten minutes, he starts playfully pretend-choking his wife. Next, the reconciliation.)

SHE: Okay, you can set the agenda this time.

HE: *(in a joking manner)*: I'd like to talk about Evelyn and why she had us leave the room. What's really going on here?

SHE: No, we're supposed to be going over what we talked about before.

HE: See, you're doing it again, you're telling me what Evelyn wants and what we're *supposed* to be doing. It's like you have this agenda all the time.

SHE: That's you, always analytical. . . .

HE: I see what happens here when we bicker. We both do the same thing, like who can get on that little piece of moral high ground first and start pushing the other one down.

SHE: No, what happens is that you pull back and tell me you want to get a divorce!

HE: No, no, that's another stage. That's when I can't win outright and I know I'm licked.

SHE: Whatever it is, it's a use of force. Not physical, but brute emotional force.

HE: No, that's a different thing. In the little bickering stuff, it's that seizing the moral high ground. Like, "I have the truth that you haven't arrived at yet, therefore I'll tell you what that is." Stylistically, we're a little different, but we both do that same thing.

SHE *(a pause, a smile)*: By the way, what did you check about how happy you are in your marriage?

HE: You really want to know? I checked "very happy."

SHE: I did too.

HE: What about, would you marry this person again?

SHE: I said "yes."

HE: Did you mean it though?

SHE *(laughing)*: Well, who else is there?

(When the therapist comes in, he says, "Could you please go away for a little longer? I'm in the middle of something here.")

This couple clearly have some fun together. And love each other. And appear to be building a workable, satisfying life. During their ten- and five-minute interludes, they look at each other, laugh a lot, and seem to be getting a kick out of each other even when they're voicing complaints or criticisms.

But she is the trusting one, the partner who displays an essentially secure style of attachment. She knows he's a fighter and clearly she doesn't entirely dislike his scrappy nature. When it crosses the line, however, and becomes an issue of concern to her—as it clearly does in the way he treats their children—she feels warranted in speaking her mind and strong enough to do so. How he is with the kids bothers her, and she pushes him to do a little better than simply acknowledge his "instinctive reactions." Something important to her is at stake and she stays with it.

He's not avoidant. He listens, he engages her on her own ground, and he talks about feelings. Yet any conclusion she comes to or interpretation she suggests, he can't accept. He will be acquiescent—yes, what you say is true—and then essentially take it back or challenge it in the next sentence—there you go again on your moral high ground. He looks at her with affection. In fact, sometimes his look suggests he finds her the juiciest woman imaginable. Yet he can get a touch nasty, and come across as if he's just picking for a fight: How about being a little more creative (in the kitchen and in the bedroom)? What is it with this need you have to impose rules and set agendas?

And apparently he's often ready to flash the ambivalent's old trump card—"I want a divorce!"

Interestingly, a touch of paranoia comes out in the reconciliation phase. Underneath his jocular remarks about what the therapist is really up to, he's a little suspicious. Worried, perhaps, about being caught out at something?

FRANK AND GIGI

Frank and Gigi have been seeing each other for two years and recently decided to pool their resources, buy a condo, and move in together. But Gigi isn't interested in lengthy discussions on the subject. When Frank starts to express his thoughts—there's an apartment that's on the small side but close to both their jobs, and another one that's more appealing but a hefty commute—Gigi is impatient. She doesn't like either of them, but says she is in love with a third place: "This apartment is perfect, but Frank insists it's overpriced. It isn't. We won't find anything like it at a lower price and he's just being pigheaded. We can afford it."

It turns out these two have spent only two Saturdays apartment hunting, and are under no pressure to move right away. But Gigi wants to get the whole business over with in a hurry. She has no patience with her boyfriend's comparative shopping and suggestion that they mull over a number of pros and cons about their choices.

Frank, a counselor with a state agency, and Gigi, a psychiatric social worker, have enjoyed a lively courtship. As they seem to be settling more and more into life "as a real couple," says Frank, they've been running into problems "about important issues—where to live, what car to buy, whose friends to hang out with. Gigi can be persuasive! She doesn't take no for an answer." Most of the time, he says, "she wears me down."

What about those friends to hang out with? we ask. How does the "no" come out there?

"He wants us to get together with his crowd all the time," Gigi says. "And I just don't like a lot of them all that much, and I don't know why he wants to spend time with them. Why don't we do things by ourselves more?"

They do, Frank insists. They go to movies and dinners and take hikes as a twosome. He's pushing, however, gently, for that broader connection. But whenever Gigi agrees to go out as part of a group, a prickly scene often ensues.

"Look," Frank says to her, "when we went to Jake and Tricia's party last week you spent half the time sitting on the couch flipping through magazines, with a black cloud over your head, and the other half getting into an argument with some guy about animal rights or something."

Gigi reiterates her opinion that these people are just not worth spending time with. "Hey," says her lover, with a smile, "they can't all be so bad! They like me and you like me, so you've got *something* in common."

WALT AND KATIE

"I cannot fathom the stubbornness, obstinacy, and really the selfishness of a forty-five-year-old man who refuses to do what he needs to do to preserve his health, when he knows what that is and when everyone's telling him he's got to do it," says Katie about Walt, her husband of fifteen years.

She's dragged him in "by the ear" to talk over the fact that although Walt has had potentially life-threatening high blood pressure for several years, he doesn't go for checkups when he should, doesn't stick with his prescription medicine, and won't adjust his diet according to the doctor's recommendations. "He's not stupid," says Katie, "so I figure he has a mental block here and needs some psychological help."

"I'm looking out for myself," says her partner, "I feel fine. I want Katie to stop all this harping at me. Pick, pick, pick."

Walter is a burly-looking, barrel-chested man who runs his own very successful construction company. The energy and charge that has his business flourishing, however, seems sometimes to get him into trouble on the home front. "He's the fighter, I'm the thinker. He's the crazy one, I'm the sane one," says Katie, impressively describing their ambivalent/secure attachment style in her own, outspoken way. "Living with Walt often takes the form of batting my head against a brick wall."

But she's clearly in love with the guy, and he looks crazy, in the nice way, about her. She was his office manager years ago, married him, then had two kids and started up a catering business, which evolved into a popular delicacies shop.

They have had many battles over the years, but Katie took the matter of his health most seriously. She was angry, because she felt he was being disloyal to his family: "We have two minor children. It seems in the final analysis, he doesn't care all that much what happens to us." In her heart of hearts, Katie knows such is not the case; in her annoyance and frustration, however, she starts sounding a bit ambivalent herself around this situation, attacking her partner's loyalty.

For his part, Walt expresses dismay at her comment: "Of course I care about my family!" he says. Then, simmering down, he says, "Look, I know Katie's right about the doctor checkups, and I'll keep at that. But on other matters, like with the kids, she's inconsistent. One day she's butting in and telling me what to feed them for lunch—remember that?" he asks his wife. "At the same time, I'm always hearing, 'Walt, you really should get more involved with the children.' How am I supposed to figure out what she wants?"

Says Katie, mildly: "I said fix them peanut butter and jelly sandwiches instead of sending for a pizza, because they eat so much of that they're going to turn *into* pizzas one day."

The issues beneath the issue here are Walt's defensiveness, drive to keep the agitation going, and lack of real desire to "figure out what she wants."

JAMES AND MERYL

After a marriage of almost twenty-three years, James and Meryl sometimes sensed they were coming to the end of the road.

"She's in retreat, she's off in the distance somewhere," says James, a show business agent, "or maybe we've retreated from each other, I don't know." They were watching longtime couples split up and old friends get divorced, and they both agree that they didn't want that to happen to them.

Meryl thinks maybe they got married too young. "We were just kids, not even out of college yet," she says. She's a downright gorgeous woman who's dressed rather severely, maybe in an effort to tone down her overall air of voluptuousness or maybe to fit her work role as corporate publications director for an accounting firm.

She says, perhaps the problem is that he has always made decisions for them, whether she liked it or not. The really big one—and the beginning of a serious rift between them—was uprooting the family from New York to move to California about six years earlier. "We talked about this and talked about it," Meryl says. "I knew James was very excited and up about the idea of joining this agency out there, but we hashed it out, over and over. I was absolutely opposed to the move; the kids had just started high school and they were miserable over the possibility of moving. As far as I was concerned, we had decided we wouldn't do it. Then he came home one night and said, 'I took the job, we're going to California.' That was it."

Although he has heard this story before, James gets his back up anew: "The kids turned out okay with it, you agreed after the fact it had helped them grow up," he says to his wife. "Besides, you loved it out there, you got into all kinds of new stuff. So what was so bad? It worked out fine."

Apparently, in many ways it did work out fine. Meryl agrees with that assessment, but shakes her head in a he-just-doesn't-get-it gesture. "I had, understandably, I think, a lot of anxiety about that move, which James simply ignored," she says. "His way of handling it was to jump in and take over." Although she marks that time as the beginning of the rift, she sees his actions then as part of a pattern that has shaped their joint life from the beginning.

She offers this example: Once, about midway through their marriage, Meryl got word that her then-job as a magazine editor was probably going to be eliminated. "I'd been at the magazine for a long time, and it was an emotional blow to think of not being there any longer," she says. "But when I told James it looked like I'd be laid off, he freaked out, which didn't help at all."

James insisted Meryl take another job the magazine was offering, although it amounted to a demotion. He called real estate agents to get estimates on their co-op, which he announced they had to sell at once. "Money was somewhat of an issue, but we weren't headed for the poorhouse," she says, "and I knew the severance I'd get would keep us in exactly the same shape for at least six months. I talked to James about all this, I said I knew losing my job had a joint impact on us, but I needed a little time to let the disruption settle and think about my next moves."

None of her analyses of their situation served to calm James down, however, and he continued to behave in a "freaked" manner. He clipped out job listings for her, called employment agencies on her behalf, and took over the household bill-paying although he wasn't especially good at it (and asked Meryl to double-check him).

All that involvement on her partner's part Meryl experienced, she says now, "as intrusive and controlling, not especially supportive." She did land another satisfactory position before those six months were up, a period during which she relied on several friends for advice and empathy. "I consider myself very fortunate in my friendships," says

Meryl. "I've got girlfriends! And the girlfriends have come through for me at crunch times."

In the last six months especially, since they've been back east, Meryl seems to be going more and more along her own road, drawing heavily on the sustenance she receives from her friends and her sisters. But it is not a road she really wishes to be on, which becomes clear over the course of several sessions.

"I don't really think James and I should or will split up," she says, and her partner looks relieved to hear those words. "The idea of being unmarried, after so long, is scary. But I just don't see much substance in the relationship anymore." Both partners admit to feeling kind of sad and lonely.

From these scenarios, do you see how outsiders often find the secure/ambivalent pair a bit of a bafflement? "Why on earth does he/she (the secure) stay with her/him (the ambivalent)?" they wonder. One is so reasonable, measured, accommodating; the other is so unreasonable, demanding, self-centered—in a word, *difficult*.

As is often the case, apparent incompatibilities don't tell the whole story.

Since ambivalents can be oppositional as well as anti-authority, they sometimes have a hard time doing what's best for themselves. Walt, for example, isn't intent mainly on ignoring his blood pressure problem; he *is* intent on rejecting the authority of doctor *and* doctor-surrogate, his wife, by not doing what they tell him to do. At the extreme, that kind of behavior can lead to drug addictions, gambling problems, or other self-destructive activities. The secure's ability to think things through clearly, express feelings, and trust will help her partner act effectively.

The ambivalent needs a lot of reassuring affection. And he is most likely to get it from a secure, who is willing to ignore the bad-boy behavior and to forgive and forget and move on.

At the same time, life with a turbulent, unpredictable ambivalent can be exciting and amusing for her steadier, feet-on-the-ground partner. Here's another relationship, besides the secure/secure, that has provided the underlying theme of many a situation comedy. Watch an *I Love Lucy* rerun, and you'll quickly identify Lucille Ball's ambivalent style: Half the time she's crazy mad, half the time, making up, while secure Ricky brings a reasoned calm to Lucy's funny, erratic antics.

Frank alludes to that appeal in talking about his family and his love of Gigi: "I was your stereotypical oldest child, the 'responsible' one. Whereas my kid brothers," he says with a laugh, "were, respectively, the borderline juvenile delinquent and the clown. Gigi has that same kind of madcap, devil-may-care quality, something I always wanted more of myself. She loosens me up."

The ambivalent is demonstrative, appreciative; with this man or woman, you've got someone who's really with you. And sex may be outstanding. Physical attraction between a secure and an ambivalent is frequently strong enough for the secure to tolerate hurtful conduct, impulsive behavior, and the push/pull attentions of the volatile mate. All that good stuff enables the secure to adapt, to build up a reservoir of positive feelings that carries the day through most of the minor turbulences.

On the other hand, the secure can feel alternately overwhelmed or deserted. His partner either wants to call all the shots or abandons all responsibility; the secure is thrown off his rails, putting great effort into keeping the partner *on* the rails, and ends up defeated much of the time. Take another look at how our ambivalent He in the opening scenario prefers to keep duking it out with his wife, rather than pay a little unemotional mind to what she's saying. Even when he acknowledges his "wrongdoing," it's with a "So what? That's just how I am" attitude.

It's easy for the secure to assume the role of intermediary and peacemaker between her partner and their children or the outside world. This is a position in which Katie often and unwillingly finds herself, and that role can be hard to sustain without losing a sense of self. Trying to bond with an ambivalent who prefers to fight is exhausting. As a protection, the secure may gradually pull back from the relationship, adopting some avoidant behaviors to keep his or her own head screwed on straight, as Meryl seems to have done in recent years. While the secure may stick with the relationship, the compromise is great and the price heavy.

TOWARD A MORE COMFORTABLE COUPLE FIT

FOR THE SECURE

Save Your Grandstand Plays for the Big Issues

Her husband, says Katie, "is worse than the kids about having his own way. What Walt wants, Walt is determined to get." She offers this example: One recent Saturday he impulsively decided they should all drive to the beach for a picnic. Katie pointed out that it seemed to be shaping up into a cool and drizzly day, and maybe they should try for the beach on Sunday. Walt insisted it would clear up, but Katie didn't think so. Walt insisted some more, and pouted, and said she was always complaining they didn't spend enough time as a family. They went to the beach—and left an hour later, wet and cold.

"When I oppose something Walt wants to get or do, he acts beyond disappointed," she says. "It's as if he had lost his best friend. It's 'How can you do this to me?' " Much of the time, she simply acquiesces: "I ask myself, is this worth the effort? Is getting my way on this important enough for what it's going to take out of me? Most of the time it's not. I save my grandstand plays for when it counts." The matter of her husband's health is clearly one that counts.

It's a sensible idea. In your own secure/ambivalent relationship, you may be sharing life with an individual who doesn't know whether she wants to serve roast beef or fish, pushes you to decide, and then chooses the opposite. Your partner most likely confronts much of the incidental business of the day with undiluted passion, arguing about it verbally and nonverbally and with an extreme sense of urgency.

And you very likely find this behavior tiring and annoying. Reduce your feelings of frustration and shore up your own boundaries by maintaining a perspective on what's important. Roast beef or fish isn't; a $300,000 apartment or a $100,000 apartment is. Give in on the first, even though it won't always feel comfortable. Katie, for example, acknowledges that sometimes she feels "taken advantage of and slightly exploited when I let Walt get his own way." But she also knows "from hard experience that I feel a lot calmer if I avoid lots of these little hassles."

Do stick to your guns about the second. If a decision will make a significant difference in your life and the lives of your mate and children, then you must fight against your partner's tendency to act impulsively, impose his or her authority, and wear you down. You must also fight against your tendency to *be* worn down and to give up trying to discuss the merits of an issue that warrants discussion.

Disengage from the Argument

Katie expressed her frustration with Walt over his inattention to his health as hitting her head against a brick wall;

she wasn't getting anywhere, despite the fact that good sense was on her side. The problem and the solution couldn't be more clear-cut—and, as she pointed out, he wasn't stupid. She was saying to her partner, "Look, you might die; you're going to leave us if you don't take proper care of yourself. We know exactly what you have to do to take proper care of yourself. How come you won't do it?"

Walt, though, a true ambivalent, detests accepting someone else's instruction; he comes out swinging. To maintain control over his life, Walt was determined to march to his own prescriptions in this matter. So he won—nobody could tell him what to do—but it was a pretty foolish victory and he knew it. Ambivalents, in their need to best the other guy, can make some abysmally poor judgments, such as not taking medicine and keeping doctor visits.

This was one of those grandstand plays for Katie. This one mattered, and she made her stand, spoke her piece, and held fast to it. But at a certain point, after all the backing and forthing, she would do well to disengage from the arguments. In that way, she can help herself feel more in control and, just possibly, get Walt to toe a line he should be toeing. When it was time for one of Walt's checkups, she might say: "I think you should go to the doctor, and if you give it some thought, I believe you'll agree. You call and make the appointment or I will. One way or the other, you'll have to go. Let me know tomorrow if you want me to make the call." Then walk away. And because he does love his family and he is a responsible man and he does know that she's right, Walt might make that call.

Katie saw the sense of this, and did pull back from the perpetual battle. And then Walt did get a little better about the whole business.

Switching gears and not allowing herself to be sucked into the argument again and again reflected a powerful—and healthy—internal shift on Katie's part. It marked a decision to go about her business and make her life; she would do what she could to encourage him toward proper action, but no longer would she constantly harp at him, acting out those more ambivalent behaviors herself.

In your own relationship, consider where and when you would be wise to stop hitting your head against a brick wall and to disengage, at least a bit. Accept the fact that your partner will never fully change—some of this is just how he is always, more or less, going to be. Remember that the ambivalent's passion is to live in chaos; to satisfy that passion, he needs to create situations that will stir up, excite, or upset his partner. Remain secure and refuse to succumb to the push for chaos, and life becomes more comfortable.

Sometimes, Act Unilaterally

It may be the only way you will get your needs met, and your needs *should* be met at times.

Frank talks about an art exhibit opening he and Gigi had attended; she was having a fine time, while he was coming down with a cold and wanted to cut the evening short. Gigi, not wishing to hear her partner's feelings because they interfered with what she wanted to do, argued: "Oh, come on, you're not tired. This is so exciting, aren't you liking this?" Frank finally announced that he was leaving whether or not she came with him. And then he left.

Frank needed to keep making those calls from time to time, as he and Gigi were moving further into their couple fit. It was becoming clear that social outings and friendships (his, hers, and theirs) were a source of friction. He was eager to start integrating her into his world a bit further, to have them become friends as a couple. It was, as we have seen, off to a rocky start.

Like many ambivalents, Gigi is prone to jealousy. Wanting her boyfriend all to herself, she becomes anxious, and her anxiety reveals itself in her resistance to his plans and suggestions. When Frank does pull her into his crowd, she often pretty quickly displays a snarky mood, either aloof or picking a fight. Then, typically, he intervenes and tries to smooth over the moment, so the evening won't turn ugly. Gigi, however, is seemingly unwilling to work at engaging or ingratiating herself with the others, so she usually jumps right back in, insists on her point, and keeps the waters roiling. They'd passed some pretty uncomfortable evenings that way.

Besides the jealousy, there is a starkly ambivalent bit of behavior afoot here. Remember that the ambivalent is frequently out of sync in social settings. When she's in, she'd rather be out; when she's out, she wants in. If the group wants her, she doesn't want the group, and vice versa. And when the group is basically the partner's group, the urge either to withdraw and go sulk in a corner or to start scrapping is heightened.

When Gigi doesn't have the full focus of her boyfriend's attention, she begins to feel that old powerlessness; she feels that unless she fights, she'll be abandoned. With unrealistic expectations of what intimacy with Frank will bring her, she expects him to tolerate her unpredictable and unreasonable outbursts over incidental or insignificant infractions on the part of others. If Frank doesn't feel like playing that game, she is quick to display sullen or hurt looks. And, typical of the ambivalent's push/pull behavior, she'd rather *he* not enjoy smooth, comfortable relationships with others, because it underlines his ability to sustain an easygoing kind of human intercourse that often eludes her. She would rather throw a little cold water on those relationships than examine her own behaviors and feelings. Sharing him is always difficult, and she has an equally tough time bringing him into her circle.

But Frank was cluing in to this pattern, starting to draw some lines, and making a few more of those unilateral decisions. There were people he wanted to see, whose friendship he would retain. On occasion he had told Gigi he would be spending an evening with friends, and he'd call her later. And on the evening he was truly sick and wanted to go home, he went home.

Acting unilaterally is a way for the secure to keep on his or her own rails, meet some personal needs, take action when the partner keeps dithering or snapping, or simply avoid lots of arguments over inconsequential matters to save energy for the grandstands that do count. There's a downside, however, to this essentially healthy bit of self-preservation. Over time, the secure, feeling worn down by and fed up with the small skirmishes or bigger battles, may come to make more and more of those unilateral decisions. He or she will even start telling the partner less and less about what he or she is up to—replacing secure behaviors with essentially avoidant ones.

Meryl was able to identify very clearly and to describe the point at which she turned the corner and started heading down a more singular road. "With James, it was always easier to give in and go along than to argue for something I wanted. He's a guy who's not quick with a 'yes!' With him, it's 'no' or 'yes, but!' And most of the time, it simply didn't matter to me. I've always believed he's basically got his head screwed on straight. I trusted him. So I was constantly weighing in my own mind what was and what wasn't worth a fight, and most of it wasn't."

Not until he made his own unilateral decision about uprooting the family and moving to California. That one was, to Meryl, worth a fight; her good judgment told her to stick with her convictions and present her case forcefully, which she did. And in fact, that should have been that. A relationship rule of thumb dictates that if one or the other partner is strongly opposed to a particular action, that action—by mutual agreement—is taken off the table. It doesn't happen. So James's abandonment of what she considered a mutually-arrived-at agreement "was kind of a final straw," she says. "After that, I developed a somewhat 'fuck it' attitude—he does what he wants, I'll do what I want."

A "fuck it" attitude turned out to make life pleasanter for her in some ways. As James rightly points out, she ended up enjoying her time on the West Coast. But the upshot, especially now that the children are grown, is that this couple has drawn apart. It took a long time and a final straw, but Meryl is a whole lot less reactive to her partner these days than she once was. She is making her own life more and more. She has left him out in many small ways, and James—like all ambivalents, acutely sensitive to how people treat him—knows it and tries even harder to reel her back in.

She relates a recent, small incident. "I've been setting up our new apartment gradually over the past couple of months. I said to James that I wanted to get something for a corner of the living room, and I'd like to buy a desk to put there, for my own use. He said, 'What for? We've got a desk in the study; you can use that when you want to. I think you ought to look for a library table for there.'

"Once, this was the kind of thing we'd go around on a couple of times, then I'd do it his way, because the argument just wasn't worth it. This time, I went out and found a desk that suited my needs and I put it right there where I wanted it."

James was upset. Faced with this fait accompli, he ranted—how could she go off and buy a desk without telling him! Intense desire for a library table was not at the heart of his ranting, of course; rather, his wife's independent action stirred up his fears of abandonment

For Meryl—and for any secure person determined to preserve and improve a relationship with an ambivalent partner that seems to be pulling apart—the challenge lies in figuring out the fine line between appropriately independent action and potentially serious disengagement from the other. It's a line you may need to consider and reconsider as you work toward a better couple fit.

Accept Apologies; Continue to Set Limits

Frank and Gigi thought they were making progress on the condo-buying front, they said during one of our sessions. Both agreed they'd take things slower and look around some more. They'd sat down and drawn up a list of agents; he'd call four and she'd call four, and they'd put together an overview of what was available. Frank made his calls; Gigi didn't.

"I told Frank I was sorry," she says, "I just didn't get around to it. But since we've decided to take our time about this, it didn't seem like such a big deal."

Gigi often tells Frank she's sorry. In fact, she usually feels deeply regretful about her poor behavior, of which she's well aware, in those social settings, and she pulls him back in with sex and apologies. That's fine—an ambivalent is capable of behaving well and also of feeling badly about behaving not so well. The secure partner, however, while accepting the apologies, must realize that the pattern may repeat. Therefore, he must continue to set limits and say "no" when a "no" is needed.

Frank tells Gigi now: "If we're serious about this apartment business, we should go at it in this sort of methodical way we've discussed. I don't want this to sound like the teacher giving the student a bad grade for not doing the homework, but that's what it feels like. You had your homework and you didn't get it done. So get it done, and then by next weekend maybe we'll have some places we want to check out."

This is a good, assertive, limit-setting statement of his feelings and expectations. If the unpleasant socializing continues, Frank may need to take a similarly clear and positive stance, and say: "Every time we go out with other people you somehow turn the evening into a nightmare. We've talked about this, it's not getting better, and I'm saying now that I'm not going to go through that all the time. I'm not going to put up with it." In putting out his own limits, he is telling his partner he expects her to regulate and contain herself in a way that they both need; he is not going to do it for her.

Understand that your own ambivalent partner is probably capable of feeling sorry about her unreasonable actions, and may be seductively eager to make amends. Accept the apology; enjoy the seductiveness. But still continue to set limits on what you will and won't tolerate. Her ambivalent attachment will not essentially change, but you can help her gain some insight into what habitually occurs between you by continuing to say "no" when "no" is necessary and not caving in to new pressures.

Soon, she may again go on the attack, but she will also be relieved that by setting clear limits you have effectively reined in some of her excesses. Contrary to appearances, she *does* want you to say "no" or "I need to address this with you." Over time, your saying "no" can help strengthen her ability to self-regulate, to give herself her own "no."

Say to Yourself at Regular Intervals, "My Partner Is Not Trying to Spite Me by Acting the Way He's Acting"

Call this your mantra, or a reminder you offer yourself every so often when pushed to accept a fresh display of your mate's less attractive behavior: the stubbornness, the opposition, the arguments, the tell-me-what-you-want-me-to-do-and-I-won't-do-it. When you function as you do along generally secure, sensible, and pragmatic lines, your partner can begin to seem as if he's simply out to spite you. What other explanation can there be, you might think, when he refuses to accept or act on what is clearly a sound decision or intellectually obvious necessity?

When Katie remarked about her husband's reluctance to tend to his medical needs, "It seems in the final analysis he doesn't care particularly what happens to his kids and to me," she was flashing a little trump card. That would bring him up short and get him paying attention, she knew, because Walt did love and feel responsible for his family. In another talk, however, she reveals a deeper feeling: "All the fussing he's done about this business seems intended just to annoy and vex me. Sometimes I wonder if he's trying to get back at me for something."

Some of that "fuck it" attitude Meryl said she had developed might be traced to her similar feeling that her partner often did what he did, not from a strong conviction about the action, but in an effort simply to rattle her cage and do the exact opposite of what she wanted.

What's important to remember here is that your ambivalent partner isn't out to be hurtful and nasty; he is looking for proof of love. Give yourself that small reminder from time to time, and then try to make hostile intentions a nonissue—take that out of the adjustments and renegotiations you are making toward a more comfortable couple fit.

In one of our sessions with Meryl and James, we asked her to talk about that uprooting of the family he perpetrated upon her, not in terms of why he did it, but as to how they handled the realities of this major couple disagreement. In some respects, each of them handled it quite well, she said, describing several ways James made the move more pleasant for her and a number of satisfactions she found about this altered lifestyle.

So, we said: "Sometimes one person does have to make a decision or take a major action that causes the partner to be unhappy. Think now, after the fact, what would have transpired, what would life have been like, if James hadn't tested those California waters? Would he look back with regret at not having made the move? Would you want him to regret not having had that opportunity?" Yes, she says, she certainly thinks he would always kick himself for not taking the job, and no, she would not want him to feel that regret. Besides, it helped him professionally, she made a good adjustment, and ultimately, she admits, things turned out all right.

This marked the beginning of a real healing process for Meryl and James, who were able to engage on a somewhat different level once the spite issue had died.

In your own relationship, you—like Meryl and most secures—probably are not a holder of grudges or keeper of scores. But perhaps a single action of your partner's, after all the minor concessions you've made along the way, is the one that seems unexplainable, except that your ambivalent mate was out to spite you. Say your mantra; let that one go.

FOR THE AMBIVALENT

Count to Ten

Katie describes her partner's "little Mt. Vesuvius eruptions" as a source of distress for one of their children: "With

Colleen, our youngest, it's water off a duck's back. Nothing bothers her. But Tyler is a sensitive kid. He takes things hard; he has a tough time dealing with his father's temper, even when it's got nothing to do with him."

One evening as the family was sitting down to dinner, a sudden downpour outside sent Walt jumping up from the table and racing around the house slamming windows, hollering, "Every goddamn window in this place is wide open! If you see it's going to rain, doesn't it dawn on anybody to check the windows and the back door?" After that outburst, Katie says, "I started talking in my cheerful, chirpy voice to settle things down, because Tyler was sitting there looking very miserable." Ten minutes later, Walt is all over his tantrum and cracking jokes. The others, however, take a while longer to return to normal.

Walt apparently, like many ambivalents, is given to flaring up with no sense of a need to limit himself or to exercise control because it's dinnertime, or the kids are there, or other people are looking unhappy. His partner assumes the role of intermediary and peacemaker, which is tiring and, in a sense, disempowering. Her husband, Katie thinks, "should try to get a better grip on himself over these little things."

Getting a better grip on yourself may be one of your biggest challenges—and one of the most immediately effective behavioral changes you can make. Just tone it down. Do not allow yourself to be set off by every small disappointment, annoyance, or failure to get your way. Do not place your partner continually in the position of playing agent of containment for your own excessive emotionality. In other words, try to adopt some of your secure partner's behaviors.

Counting to ten, backing off, or just dropping it will be difficult, but give it a try. When you know you are about to jump on the same old merry-go-round, say, "I better not get into this anymore right now. I love you." And walk away.

When an instant resolution to a problem is not forthcoming, let it be and come back to it later.

Give Up Tit-for-Tat

With the ambivalent, there is always bargaining; if he has to give up this, he'll take up that (I'll stop with the cigarettes and start with the cigars). The ambivalent keeps that scorecard going, and attempts to draw the partner into bargaining mode.

Secure Frank asks his ambivalent girlfriend to spend an evening out with friends. Gigi agrees, then allows neither Frank nor herself to enjoy it. That's her tit-for-tat: You'll get your evening but I'll make you pay for it.

"Could you pick one couple you think you could like," we ask her, "and decide that with just these people, for just this night, you'll have a good time? And if that doesn't pan out too successfully, try again with some others?" She could do that, she thinks; and she did. After two such greatly more successful social get-togethers, Gigi had proof that she could change one piece of behavior (for a while, at least) and that she could indeed contain her feelings to a greater degree; she need not be so swamped by anxiety, jealousy, and fear of abandonment. That accomplishment freed her to the possibility of real insight, to the point where she was able to recognize and talk about some of that tit-for-tat she habitually extracted from her boyfriend.

Try to spot your own bargaining tendencies. Put down the scorecard.

Don't Make Up Through Sex

Ambivalents, in our professional experience, are sexual hotheads; they especially relish sex after a physical separation or after an emotional one like a fight. It's how they reconnect, and they can reconnect on a dime.

For Frank and Gigi, sex was great. Part of the pull and appeal tied in to the fact that they maintained their separate apartments, got together every three nights or so when he'd sleep over at her place or she at his, and on weekends. All that separating and reuniting was intensely sexy—Gigi talked about calling Frank one midnight, needing to be with him, rushing over there in a cab, "wanting to jump his bones as soon as he opened the door."

That passion won't necessarily lessen once they set up housekeeping together. The ambivalent doesn't generally pull back sexually, as the avoidant will. But Gigi will continue to push and pull, keep things stirred up, through the arguments over the friends or the furniture or the weekend plans or whatever else. Hotheadedness keeps her pumped up *and* feeling sexual, because of the powerful link between aggressive feelings and sexual feelings. And her partner probably loves all that intensity, *but* over time, as the relationship grows and becomes more deeply intimate, he may weary of the love-bunny-followed-by-the-termagant displays. Quite possibly, these two will become sexually out of sync—and then one of the major attractions of the ambivalent/secure couple fades.

Don't make up through sex, or at least, not right away. When you *do* lose it and blow up, strive immediately afterward for a neutral cooling-off period rather than the instant, passionate reconciliation. As an ambivalent, you are likely to switch to the all-loving seducer once your black mood passes. But in your efforts to forge a better couple fit, you need to be working at tempering both those all-or-nothing extremes.

We're not saying lose the passion, but rather, stretch a little. You can have both. The making up in the bedroom is lovely, but you need to remember it doesn't signify a problem resolved; allow the sex, perhaps, to soften the mood for further and rational exploration of an issue that's not over and done with just because you got your partner to make love to you.

Emote Somewhat Less; Intellectualize Somewhat More

As we will point out elsewhere, the ambivalent can act more productively and thoughtfully when he shifts from the emotional to the intellectual mode. An intellectual stock taking in a broader sense and a coolheaded and clear-eyed analysis of the strengths of the relationship can help the ambivalent get a better grip on himself—and thus see the value of struggling toward that better fit.

James—with his back against the wall now, fearing the possible dissolution of his marriage—started thinking hard about what he had, what he wanted, and what role he had played in his partner's drawing apart. Once he started thinking, he was dead sure of one thing: He wanted to keep his wife. That was his bottom line. That was also the beginning of a real turnaround, the point at which he was able and willing to work at keeping issues in perspective.

It's better not to wait until your back is against the wall. Consider the aspects of your relationship that matter to you. You may find it a useful exercise, in fact, to write them down, and reflect on the history behind them. In counseling a couple who seem to present only a full plate of grievances and differences, we search for points of connection, the shared values. We listen for "us" and "we"—"Getting the kids through college is the most important thing to us," "We always wanted to live way out in the country," "We don't believe in divorce."

Think about your own "us" and "we." If there are at least

a few of them, you have a foundation on which to build and change.

Say to Yourself at Regular Intervals, "Not Getting What I Want from My Partner Does Not Mean My Partner Doesn't Love Me"

For the ambivalent, not getting what she wants signifies at some deep level a loss of autonomy and love. All the hammering away at the other is the ambivalent's means of getting self-affirmation and the reassurance that she will not be abandoned by the object of her affection. Remember what we said earlier about the ambivalent child's failure, for whatever combination of unique circumstances, to sense his own power, his ability to influence the caretaker to come when needed or wanted. Learning at an early age that one can influence events marks the beginning of autonomy. The ambivalent never achieved that knowledge, and so as an adult she is a bit of an empty vessel. With not much independence to build on, the ambivalent is always in a sense starting from scratch: Prove it to me again that I can influence you to do what I want (to love me).

So here is a simple sounding but powerful truth, one that it is hard for you to accept. Make it your mantra: When I don't get what I want, it doesn't mean my partner doesn't love me.

CHAPTER 10

Ships That Pass in the Night:
The Avoidant/Avoidant Couple

HE AND SHE

THIS young, newly married couple clearly enjoyed being in each other's company and had no trouble keeping the talk going for their allotted minutes. Both articulate, they gave off at the same time a subdued, somewhat professorial air, especially him. Holding our list, and keeping his eyes fixed on it ninety percent of the time, he started things off.

HE: Okay, first—"decisions about spending money." Money responsibility.

SHE: Okay. You tend to be more in control of how we spend money, I guess wisely so, since I'm more impulsive. You like to keep me a little in the dark. He's in charge of the books.

HE: Well, I think that's basically true. But my major complaint with Ellen is that I'd like to be able to go over the records with her on a monthly basis, so she would have a better sense of where the money goes. Otherwise, I think we're pretty much in line with our values overall about how we spend.

SHE: Yes. But I'm just not all that interested in going over it on a monthly basis. That's why he does it.

HE: True. But I guess I feel I'd like to have that burden shared. I'd do the paperwork, as now, but I'd like to think she knew more precisely where our money was going, in a more timely fashion.

SHE: You're right, especially since I'm going to be spending most of it!

HE: Second . . . "personal time."

SHE: This is more your issue, I'd say.

HE: Okay . . . well, we've recently had a baby, so obviously that cuts into everybody's time. But I know for myself, I would like a little more personal time to pursue my own hobbies. I'm sort of individualistic, I have . . .

SHE: Single-person hobbies.

HE: Yes, single-person hobbies, and so since I work hard during the week, I'd like to carve out some weekend time for myself. Plus, I think since we both work and Ellen also has the major responsibility for the baby, I think she'd like to have more time with me, and I'm carving into that when I claim time for my own interests.

SHE: Well, I work, and then if I want to do things during the day with some friends that wouldn't include Bob, I do that, so I don't need so much more time just to be by myself. But I would like to spend more weekend time with Bob and I'd also like him to spend more time with Trisha. But I think that's gotten better lately, don't you?

HE: One thing we've tried to talk about in the past is

hobbies and sports we could do together, and it just hasn't really worked out. Because of who I am, I'm somebody who likes to go at very technical or demanding types of activity, and that doesn't always have room for other people.

SHE: Yeah, I'd like to do more sports and it would be nice if Bob could do them with me, but it just doesn't seem to . . . But we share the same interests and I do sometimes hang out and comment on what he's doing. . . . But a lot of it is one-person stuff, like I couldn't be in the darkroom with you.

HE: I'm into photography. . . . I guess we covered this.

SHE: You think so? Well, the one thing is—and we've both said this—I wish we did have a hobby we could do together. But who would take care of the baby?

HE: Yes, but even before the baby, we struggled with this. I think part of it is I tend to be very gung ho about things and Ellen is less so. So we'll pick something out and I get into it and stick with it and develop a certain expertise, and Ellen goes off to pursue something else. I mean, not that one way is better than the other, it's just that I will get into something that doesn't lend itself to two people working at it at once.

SHE: Yeah, that's true.

HE: All right, next . . . "showing appreciation and affection." I don't want to speak for Ellen, but for myself I think we're right on the money with that.

SHE: Absolutely. We couldn't appreciate each other more. Well, maybe in terms of showing affection . . . Sometimes I think, when Bob and I first got together, I was less of a team player, more self-centered. And I didn't contribute as much, just in terms of chores and the things that need to get done when you live with somebody. I think I've improved, but sometimes I wonder if to you I'm still stuck in my former incarnation. I think I could get more credit for what I do now. For how I've improved, in other words.

HE: Well, I think what Ellen is talking about goes back to my cracking the whip in the early stages of our being together. It was about the practical aspects of a marriage, and I think Ellen is more appreciative of that now.

SHE: Yes, the chores.

HE: Yeah, the maintenance aspects of a marriage and a household. That wasn't so true earlier on, and I used to feel that . . .

SHE: You were pissed. And you were right to be pissed. But sometimes now when Bob gets annoyed about something, he acts as if I'm still the way I used to be and I don't think I am that way anymore.

HE: Well, I don't think that's so true.

SHE: Well, okay.

HE: Four—"expressing emotions." Again, I think we're right on about that. We have no problems, like with yelling at one another. *(They laugh.)*

SHE: True.

HE: I think we run the whole gamut, from joy to sadness.

SHE: And anger.

HE: And anger. If there's any kind of downside here, I think it's that we overexpress our emotions.

SHE: That's true.

HE: I guess the main issue is spending more time together.

SHE: Yes, well I think that will get better when the baby gets older. Although, no, that's not the point, because we're going to have more children, I hope, not less children in the future. Right now, I have to get more comfortable with going out and leaving the baby. I feel the time I do have I want to spend with her. Bob and I don't spend a lot of time together, and not just time alone together, but going out with other people. We don't do that much anymore.

HE: Actually, we probably spend more time together than most couples. Maybe Ellen won't agree with this, but we're both professionals and our jobs are such that we're more fortunate than some of our peers in being able to arrange our hours. When I look at some of my friends with not so much flexibility, I'm grateful that we have as much leeway as we do.

SHE: That's true.

HE: We both in our individual jobs have a lot of flexibility, which at least in my profession is unprecedented, and I think we take this for granted frankly. I'm not sure we need more time together. . . . Maybe it's the way we spend our time. . . . I mean, everyone can always use more time.

(Ten minutes are up, followed by the reconciliation.)

HE: We can talk about anything? *(He puts the list down on the table, turns for the first time this afternoon to face her. There's a lengthy pause.)* This is harder! Well, we can do what we always do and talk about how our respective days were. . . . Our relationship?

SHE: No.

HE: You don't want to talk about our relationship? Well, okay, I'll begin. Okay, here's something—my observations, as I was going through those handouts, and as I was reflecting on what was being asked of me about my relationship, which you don't tend to often analyze in that quantitative way. And I found that for the most part, my answers were on the positive side.

SHE: Me too.

HE: Almost to the point where I wanted to answer "unbelievably happy" and "never have thought about not being married," although I felt I had to knock it down one level just to sound realistic.

(She laughs.)

SHE: I want to ask you a question. On the sheet where it said, "When disagreements arise, they usually result in the husband giving in or the wife giving in or agreement by mutual give and take," what did you answer?

HE: I put mutual give and take.

SHE: You're kidding! I thought you'd say you always give in.

HE: That's only when I'm going to lose.

(They laugh.)

HE: No, really, I think I give in a lot and you give in too, I'd say there's mutual give and take.

(After some more talk about giving and taking, time is up.)

This He and She come across as solidly content with each other and with their marriage. Life, we get the impression, runs pretty smoothly; although they refer to all that "yelling" they do, we'd guess not a great deal of it actually goes on.

He remains calm, cool, and collected as he goes down the list, ticking off each item as if these were points on an outline of a history paper. Even talking about how "unbelievably happy" he is in their relationship, his voice is distant and uninflected. He establishes a methodical, intellectualized approach to their discussion, and she follows suit.

There is not a great deal of real interaction, and at times they seem to carry on almost as if the other were not present, each referring to his or her partner in the third person, as "he" or "Bob," "she" or "Ellen." A few issues start percolating in just the barest way—he thinks she doesn't pay enough attention to the family finances; she thinks he is hanging out in that darkroom too much; he thinks she poops out of their joint extracurricular activities; she thinks he doesn't acknowledge her improved involvement in chores. And does she want more appreciation or more affection or both?

But the heat gets turned off and they let those matters drop without much engagement—he by outtalking her and assuming a slightly superior or dominant position, she by agreeing with his reassessments.

VINCENT AND ELIZABETH

Here we have Vincent, a vice-president in a manufacturing concern, and Elizabeth, his wife of twelve years and a stay-at-home mom to their three children. And here we have a classic case of a straw breaking an avoidant camel's back.

"What brings you here?" we ask at their first session, and Elizabeth describes the following straw: They had recently attended the wedding of a longtime pal of Vincent's, a fraternity brother embarking on marriage for the first time at age forty-two. At the reception, Vincent and three other best buddies from those college days rose, one by one, to toast newlywed Kevin and his bride. And each of "the boys" poked a little lighthearted fun at Kevin's long bachelorhood and ended their toasts with straight-from-the-heart remarks about the great joys and deep comforts that they were sure lay ahead for their friend.

"After ten years as a married man," said one, "I can tell you, Kev, that it only gets better." "We all thought this day would never come," said another, "but then our old bud met the love of his life and went down like a ton of bricks, like I did when my gorgeous Allison here came along, and Kev, if you and Jen are half as happy as we've been, you're a lucky guy." And so on. Vincent was the last to speak. He made some amusing references to the good old, bad old times back in the frat house, spoke of Kevin's virtues as a loyal friend and his smarts as an investment counselor, and wished the couple all the best. No mention of Elizabeth or their marriage.

She was stunned, embarrassed, and badly hurt, watching the other women beaming up at their loving husbands. Driving home with Vincent after the reception, she spoke up: "How could you have totally left me out of your remarks? Everybody except you mentioned their wives. It was as if I didn't exist."

The evening was a watershed; suddenly, Elizabeth realized she and Vincent don't really connect. She also realized that she'd known it for a long time, and that she couldn't bury that knowledge anymore. She broke her avoidant pattern and, most uncharacteristically, acknowledged to him her unhappiness—how could you have done that? Vincent, shocked, was silent. Three days later, she'd found a marriage counselor, made an appointment, and sat before us with her uncomfortable but determined-looking husband.

This attractive couple both say they have a wonderful marriage and great kids. He's a wonderful husband and a wonderful father, she says. She's a wonderful wife and a wonderful mother, he says. If all is so fine, we can't help asking, how come life feels pretty rotten at the moment? They are not sure. They just think they "need to communicate better."

In their vague references to "better communication," Vincent and Elizabeth are typical avoidants, individuals who engage in a great deal of denial. The avoidant couple will have a hard time pinpointing exactly what's wrong; they know *something* is amiss, but it's all pretty nebulous. When pressed for a fuller explanation, Elizabeth says that occasionally days go by when he's not talking at all. She assumes there's a problem, and she doesn't understand how he fails to see that she's upset. Says Vincent: "Well, I do start to notice she's unusually quiet, and I wonder, 'What did I do now?'" Finally, this whole undercover scenario gets on the nerves of one or the other, and he or she blurts out, "Okay, what's the matter with you?" Before then, the silent mode may have prevailed for a week.

It takes several sessions before these two begin to reveal other problems at the core of their discontent and distance from each other. For one thing, they rarely have sex any longer.

NATE AND ELENA

Nate and Elena are feeling fairly comfortable at the moment, after a long, frazzled year. Nate, a computer programmer, and Elena, a speechwriter for a major communications company, had been big spenders since their marriage three years ago. Even before then, each tended to pay out more than was coming in.

When Nate's job was cut to part-time and Elena learned her job would be phased out before the end of the year, this couple carried on as before. They ate out most evenings, while

Nate continued to add to his CD jazz collection and Elena kept up her twice-weekly workouts at a private gym, all the time saying nothing and watching each other continue to spend. Only when bankruptcy seemed a possibility did they manage to cut down on expenses and put their financial lives on track. And once both connected with new (although still only temporary) jobs, they decided on some short-term counseling. The events of the past year had given them a real scare.

As they talk, Elena, in particular, begins to put her finger on general areas of dissatisfaction. For example, she says: "Nate has always been absorbed in his love of music and bridge. When he's not involved in either of those, he's at his computer. I always got the feeling he didn't seem to want to spend time with me."

Once, she told Nate how she felt, and his first response was defensive: "Sure, I like spending time with you," he said, and then asked if she wanted to come with him to his next bridge tournament. This wasn't what Elena had in mind.

In the way they denied their anxieties and were unwilling to confront or even think about their troubled money situation, Nate and Elena were behaving like typical avoidants. Skirting conflict is the primary goal here, for deep in the heart of an avoidant is the fear that conflict will lead to abandonment.

The avoidant's M.O.: Ignore the problem and it will go away; if it doesn't, handle it on your own.

PAMELA AND MATT

Pamela is a lawyer in her mid-thirties. Matt, forty-one, is a doctor. Neither has been married or engaged or even had a long-term steady. They were introduced by mutual friends over a year ago, genuinely enjoyed each other's company at once, and have been spending much time together. They've fallen, or are falling, in love. They're nervous!

In a rather unusual, quite delightful development, about five months ago Matt decided he could use a little help moving forward in his love life. He found himself a therapist, and seems to be making a determined effort to overcome his avoidant tendencies and connect with this lovely lawyer. And make her his wife.

He's told Pamela a bit about some past relationships that never took off; he talks about his love of kids and his desire to start a home. Lately, he's been asking her opinion a lot, too: What does she think about this new suit he bought? Should he get a bigger car? He seems to be moving ever further into more open and personally revealing behaviors toward the object of his affection.

It has all had an effect on Pamela, who was inspired to look us up, do some talking, and get some counseling herself—because she, too, really does wish to move forward, possibly into married life with this man she does love and admire. But moving forward in a romantic relationship, she knows, has historically eluded her. She wants some help. She doesn't want to mess this one up.

If you recall F. Scott Fitzgerald's novel *The Great Gatsby*, or you saw the movie with Mia Farrow as Daisy Buchanan and Bruce Dern as her husband Tom, you'll peg Daisy and Tom as two avoidants. Daisy ignores clear evidence that Tom is having an affair with the sensual wife of the garage owner. When Daisy begins a flirtation with the mysterious Jay Gatsby, Tom shows no awareness of it. The Buchanans feel that any display of emotion is unreal, permitting them to treat relationships as if they had no meaning. In their denial and distortion of reality, they destroy the lives of their lovers.

The avoidant/avoidant couple is actually a somewhat rare breed, since two avoidants tend not to hook up with each other. When they do, and problems loom, it's difficult to get them to counseling. It takes the straw on the camel's back or the major scare or a love-motivated wish to be something different to get them to start talking about themselves. Once in counseling, they often discover that the going gets tougher and more painful the longer they stick with it, and they frequently don't stick with it very long.

At their second session, for example, we suggested to Vincent and Elizabeth that we meet once a week for a while and see how things went. Vincent was all for it, saying, "Fine, whatever it takes to do this." By the fourth session, however, he'd changed his tune: "I don't know if meeting every week is such a great idea. Maybe once a month or on an as-needed basis." Elizabeth nodded in agreement, although more tentatively. She was nervous about upsetting the marriage; he was nervous about dropping his armor. Something had to give, and that's a threatening prospect for the avoidant/avoidant couple.

Typically, two avoidants get together when one pursues the other, rather than because of sexual attraction. They may share interests. Or maybe the chase is on because of a special quality to admire—he's the smartest man I've ever met or she's the kindest woman I've ever known. Possibly the attraction is that the other person *is* avoidant, a bit unavailable or distant, as was the case for Pamela. Although it developed that Matt would be doing the pursuing, Pamela initially felt the bigger attraction and took the initiatives, not in least part because he didn't come tapping at her all the time with this or that. He gave her a lot of freedom and he liked her independence.

These avoidant approaches are not necessarily bad. The pursuer is attracted to the special, admirable quality and then the pursuee opens up a bit, likes being liked for his virtues, and can trust the other. This is how two avoidants become a pair.

And it can be a perfectly well-functioning pairing. When life is perking along smoothly and includes focused activities and goals, these two can do very well. They may enjoy each other's strengths and still maintain a distance that feels comfortable.

New situations don't overwhelm avoidants. If jobs, a military career perhaps, require this couple to move frequently, for example, they'll settle into new environments with ease. Small conflicts are dealt with on an intellectual level, which isn't so bad. They can talk—dispassionately, perhaps, but cool talk is better than no talk at all.

When tough problems loom, however, the Vincent and Elizabeths, Nate and Elenas, Pamela and Matts of the world have a hard time taking joint action. Each will try to get past the hurdles by making independent decisions, and this is rarely the best way to go.

Even when all is calm, the emotional chill in the relationship may take its toll as time passes. When two avoidants slowly, inexorably drift apart, without acknowledging the widening gulf between them, one—like Elizabeth—can begin to feel dangerously depressed and forlorn. Original attractions become irritants. One or both may start voicing small criticisms, and these are people who can't bear to be criticized. They take it hard. They may not fight, but they will be hurt and angry, and eventually stop talking.

And then one day a bolt from the blue in the form of a major relationship or family crisis knocks one or the other, sometimes both, into a realization that they have been co-existing as two ships passing in the night. In a time of unusual need, the partner is not quite available. Or even without the bolt from the blue, a day may dawn when they look at each other and perceive the depths of their discontent: Suddenly, she's boring; she's not the woman he married. Suddenly, he's nasty; he's not the man she married. But of course they are—each was just all dressed up back then.

Each partner in the avoidant/avoidant relationship can feel a whole lot better—happier, more loved, and less lonely—if each risks helping and feeling for the other.

TOWARD A MORE COMFORTABLE COUPLE FIT

Listen to Your Emotions

Now, obviously, we all would be wise to listen to our emotions, but avoidants have an especially hard time hearing the voices coming forth from that well. *Thinking*, they think, is what they are good at.

We tell avoidants that's fine, and there's much to be appreciated about a cautious, intellectual style. In fact, however—and this comes as news to our couples—you two are even better at *feeling*. Your thinking tends to be a bit convoluted or skewed at times; you adhere to rigid positions. (You're the man or woman who finds a dentist, dislikes him on sight, then keeps seeing him for the next twenty years.) But your feelings, by and large, are strongly intuitive, and real. Try to hear them. Listen to your emotions; rely on your intuitions.

Consider our avoidant/avoidant couples. Each individual is a veritable hothouse of emotion! Vincent is dismayed by his wife's unhappiness and furious that it has something to do with him. Elizabeth longs for affection and appreciation. Nate and Elena, until recently, were filled with anxiety over jobs and money, and they're still not out of the woods. Pamela's afraid of falling in love, and afraid not to. As much as possible, however, they avoid *feeling* those feelings, and certainly would rather not discuss them with their partners. Avoidants tend neither to give nor to expect emotional support; they learned long ago to manage sadness, loneliness, anxiety, or fear without help from others.

Much of the time, they prefer to stay in their heads. Talking about the communications job she recently lost, Elena thinks she might have been in a stronger position had she accepted one of two previous promotions she had been offered. "I spent too much time thinking it over," she says now. "But I was never sure that those new positions would be the right move. There were several factors mitigating against taking the promotions." Weighing those mitigating factors certainly was wise. But without also trusting her gut instincts, she was powerless to act; she could never reach a clear "yes" or "no."

Use your head, by all means, but your heart as well. At times of change or decision, ask yourself, "Does this feel right?" in addition to, "Does this make sense?" As you become keener at listening to your emotions, you will find it more and more difficult to avoid them (if not yet awfully easy to act on them). You simply can't keep that evasion going any longer, which is all to the good. A certain clarity is dawning.

Send Clear Signals, Preferably by Stating Your Thoughts and Wishes

Once you have tuned in to those emotions and intuitions, push yourself to express them. Avoidant/avoidant couples are dreadful at sending and receiving signals, and at saying what they want and need. Each prays that the other, through some kind of osmosis, will simply "get it."

When Pamela, the lawyer falling in love with the doctor

who was falling in love with her, heard from Matt that he would be attending his twentieth college reunion at Dartmouth, she dearly wanted to go with him. She wished he would ask her, and felt left out when he didn't. However, she clued him in on none of this, even though he had already taken her to a number of his social affairs, including a holiday party for his hospital staff, evenings out with his friends, and a dinner with his sister when she was in town.

We ask Pamela: "What are you waiting for? Let him know how you feel. You are not going to invite yourself to the reunion; that's not your style. But why not tell him just what you told us? You're going to miss him all weekend. You'd enjoy being in on the fun. Ask! Talk!" She did ask, but with a great deal of angst. And he was delighted, immediately invited her to come along with him, and had a plane ticket for her the next day. He told her that he hadn't been sure she would want to be asked (Matt still shows some avoidant colors, such as waiting for his partner's go-ahead signal).

Pamela was tickled pink. She had been afraid that he didn't want her to be seen as "the girlfriend," or that he wanted to be away from her for a while (the old abandonment issues surfacing). She was also afraid to show him that she really cares a lot. And although she returned from that trip with reports that all went well, she remains hesitant about inviting her beau further into her circle. "You think I should bring him out to my beach house share some weekend?" she asks. "That's a mixed bag of people. I don't know if my friends will like him all that much." In her fear of moving further and further into intimacy, she invents obstacles and turns a blind eye to the obvious reality that her adult friends are unlikely to comment on her relationship and probably would find this fellow just fine anyway.

Pamela is going to have to work at developing a sense of greater comfort in closeness—speaking up, sharing information about herself with her boyfriend, and peeling away the layers of the onion so she is more clearly revealed. All of these are skills she never had an opportunity to practice in her family. "That was a quiet household," she says. "It seems we all just never told each other very much." As it turned out, her family went beyond quiet into downright secretive. After her mother died two years earlier, Pamela learned that both her parents had previously been married, and that her father's first marriage produced a son whom he hadn't seen since shortly after the boy's birth.

She was stunned, then angry, and is still coming to terms with the fact that both her parents were essentially enigmas. She wonders if and how she might establish contact with that unknown half-brother. But uppermost in her mind is the wish to be less reserved and more communicative with this man who will almost surely become her husband. "It's hard for me to talk about myself, especially about my feelings," she says. "In my family, you weren't supposed to *have* feelings, certainly not unpleasant ones. My mother would become nervous and annoyed if I went around looking sad or unhappy. She'd say, 'Come on, snap out of it, it's a beautiful day.' As if one didn't have the right to feel sad."

Speaking one's piece is a mouthful for an avoidant. Sometimes it doesn't come out right. Vincent, for example, one day abruptly said to Elizabeth, "Why don't you get a babysitter once in a while and get out of the house more?" Elizabeth heard this question as a criticism of her (she was turning into a bore, a house mouse, too involved with the kids and they'd do just as well in some other woman's care) and she angrily rejected his suggestion. And so Elizabeth and Vincent each pulled back into their separate huts and let the matter drop.

In our session, Vincent acknowledges that he can be critical, and he guesses his remark was sort of a criticism of his wife, because she's always caught up with the kids and the house and she seems like a gloomy Gus a lot of the time. He also thinks she has a lot on her plate and there is no question they can afford some babysitting help. "But I never know how to say things to Liz," he says. We offer a suggestion: "Sit down with her and say, 'Look, what do you think? You're the one staying home, you've got three kids all day. This is too much. I think we should figure out how to let you get more of a break.' "

He saw the need for a change in tone from accusatory to empathetic. If the lesson takes, he may handle the next incident with greater understanding. Or not. Although they may agree with the counselor's observation and suggestion ("Oh yes, you're absolutely right"), avoidants don't typically experience a floodgate of insight; it's only a small window that opens.

Keep the window open. Work at saying, without criticism, what you think, want, and need. It is okay to be angry, and to say so, and to say why. You can tolerate it. Your avoidant partner can and will respond. If only for the sake of dodging conflict and keeping the peace, he or she will attempt to meet reasonable demands.

Practice Making Joint Decisions

Although Nate and Elena are not desperately unhappy with the small suburban condo they bought when they married, neither are they especially pleased with it, each for his or her own reasons. Says Nate: "The place is badly designed, just what these slap-it-up quick builders think yuppie couples want. A huge bathroom with a Jacuzzi tub, all kinds of fancy lighting, a sink counter that runs the length of the wall. A master bedroom with a deck, which we never use. Then, a dinky second bedroom, a living room with a pretentiously beamed and angled ceiling, thin walls throughout." There is no good space for his stereo system or his computer station.

Elena complains, "I never wanted to live in one of these bedroom communities. The places all look the same, and there's too much upkeep on this house for what we get out of it." She doesn't like being so dependent on her car either.

So, we ask, "How did you both come at the decision to buy your home?"

"I don't know," says Elena. "We end up doing a lot of things we're unhappy about. It seems we never discuss anything for more than two seconds. I don't think either of us cared that much about where we lived."

These two are suffering the consequences, if mildly, of their inability to make joint decisions. They have difficulty remembering that they're on the same team, and that it behooves them to talk out personal needs and preferences. They go along their separate paths, or decide they "don't care" which way a particular ball bounces. Restricted by their avoidant tendencies, they get themselves in hot water when a really damaging issue, like lack of money, arises. They need to practice making more of those joint decisions, starting small.

You and your avoidant partner are probably right now dividing up the household business: He takes care of vacation plans; you take care of dinner plans. He buys the gas; you buy the IRAs.

This can be a sensible approach to life. Dividing up decisions and responsibilities is what couples do; it's efficient. Watch a man and woman trundling a shopping cart around the supermarket together, and you figure either this pair has a pathetic need never to be apart or they haven't worked out some good ways not to duplicate simple efforts. But you and your partner can get too good at going it alone. And sooner or later, a life event will demand truly joint engagement.

Better to dabble in a little more engagement now and get the hang of it, rather than wait until a crisis or explosion.

Practice being a team. Say: "You know, we ought to be thinking of leasing a new car. I saw some good rates. Let's talk it over tonight." Say: "I've been taking care of our investments, as we know. Now I'm going to come to you regularly and we'll just talk over what I've been doing." If your partner replies, "Well, I don't know, that's not my expertise, you make the decisions," reply in turn: "That's okay, I'll continue doing so. But we'll just talk it over, I just want to keep you informed."

Joint decisions might involve the daily minutiae. Two avoidants, uncomfortable with the hour-by-hour interactions, will often deal poorly with these small realities of life. They may play dumb. One man we know had agreed with his wife that he would take on the job of making their bed every morning, no problem; then he said he didn't know how. Since this fellow had spent two years in the army, we might assume that the act of tucking in sheets would not, in fact, pose any difficulty.

It's not the case that two avoidants attempting to implement joint task-takings don't know *how* to make the beds, stack the dishwasher, or write the checks. They just back off from the doing, because performing the actions means giving to the other, and drawing closer in mundane ways. Distance is their preferred style. Interestingly, avoidants are generally good at solving problems. The behaviors come out not in their business or professional lives, but in the intimate situations that constitute the practical underpinnings of the relationship.

The idea is to engage in regular back-and-forth. It's a skill you should develop, because sooner or later something big is going to drop into your lives that will require combined, concerted attention. Learn how to handle different cards because you won't be able to play every hand the same way.

Engage in (at Least) One Joint Activity

Our He and She couple at the start of this chapter were actually onto a good idea about those hobbies or sports they thought they ought to be doing more of together. Two avoidants do well, and actually feel quite pleased with themselves and each other, when they are focused on common activities or goals.

Nate and Elena had stumbled into one of those in the past year, when much of their life seemed to be unraveling, and both acknowledged it was a source of real, mutual satisfaction. They planted a small vegetable garden behind their condo (there was, perhaps, some subconscious notion here of achieving a greater degree of self-sufficiency, living off their carrots and tomatoes if all else failed!). They got into it. They loved it. They enjoyed working together on it. In fact, they've hatched bigger and better plans for next summer's garden.

We can see that this activity allowed them to work in concert. They liked each other's commitment and efforts, yet maintained a comfortable distance. Digging around together in the earth, weeding and reaping, together but in a side-by-side, looking-elsewhere sort of way, turned out to enhance their feelings of satisfaction as individuals and in their relationship.

Hug and Kiss More

Not a whole lot of hugging and kissing goes on between avoidant pairs. Each individual seems to feel depleted by the giving of a kiss or a hug, as if he or she had only a limited supply of such small demonstrations of affection. You need to replace feelings of depletion by ones of replenishment. Replenishment is a simple idea: By giving, you get. Offer a hug and a kiss and you invite, essentially demand, a response; get a hug and a kiss back and you'll be encouraged to give more. A process is underway.

Hugging and kissing, of course, is part of connecting sexually in any romantic relationship. Some avoidants don't perceive that, however.

The longer she talks, the more Elena is able to reveal the deep, physical loneliness she experiences in her marriage. She begins by saying, obliquely, that Nate "isn't very affectionate." Encouraged by the counselor, Elena expresses a wish for "more cuddling" in bed, then says something that brings Nate's head snapping around to stare at her—she had been worrying lately that he might be having an affair. Of course he's not having an affair, he insists, then adds: "You're sexually satisfied, I know that. So am I. I guess we do just get right down to business when we're having sex, but you know, a lot of the time it's late, we're both tired. Neither one of us wants a lot of fooling around."

We had come an admirably long way from discussing exclusively this couple's sometimes destructive financial habits. Certainly, it seemed appropriate to suggest that some more of that "fooling around" might help Elena to feel less deserted by her partner.

Unsurprisingly, sex frequently looms as a biggie for avoidant pairs. Physical intimacy disappears fast from the relationship. These two can enjoy sex, but they are more greatly satisfied over time with other qualities in each other; they aim subconsciously at reaching and sustaining a feeling of comfortable companionship. They're not, we might say, sufficiently aggressive to summon up sexual passions—all feelings are so tamped down that the urges just don't come.

Early in the courtship when love is high, being sexually active isn't usually a problem. But the longer and more genuinely intimate the relationship becomes, the more each partner's energies and urges flow into staying quiet, calm, and essentially isolated from the other.

But a lack of sex is a symptom, a by-product of the lack of overall intimacy. If you haven't slept with your partner in a month, something's wrong.

Vincent and Elizabeth had not had sexual relations in weeks (she acknowledges this with embarrassment, when we ask, "How's your sex life?" and we did have to ask because they would never bring up the issue and because sex does matter). This couple can't discuss sex any better than they can any other troublesome matter, but they need to give it a try—the talking, at least. Have you and Vincent *talked* about it? we ask Elizabeth. They have not, she tells us. We ask, Would you be able to say to him at some point after a long dry spell in the bedroom, simply this: "We haven't slept together in a long time"? "I guess I could do that," she says. That's a step forward, a start.

Quite possibly, raising the observation will go nowhere. Your partner might reply, "Gee, you're right," and then you both let the matter thud into oblivion. But at least you've put it, briefly, on the table. You've observed, in so many words, that something important isn't happening. Couples who have let sexual passion fade—and we suggested as much to Elizabeth and Vincent—can try to recall the early feelings, when they first got together; how good and pleasing, perhaps, the sexual connection was back then. And how they might attempt to recapture some of that comfort in intimacy.

Which brings us back to the hugging and kissing. Avoidants feel squeamish about being demonstrative; even if you have no problems in bed, chances are you seldom engage in small spontaneous displays of affection.

You should. More physical contact will warm the cool atmosphere that prevails in your twosome. Touching without necessarily having sex is a useful activity; it takes the pressure off. Also, it can help decrease the possibility that one or both of you loses interest entirely in fanning the dying sexual embers of your relationship and will become vulnerable to outside romantic temptations.

Here's a simple exercise: Share a serious kiss, instead of a quick peck on the cheek, before heading your separate ways each morning. Give each other a thirty-second hug each evening when you reconnect. (When you first try this, thirty seconds will feel like forever, but just hang on.)

Stay in the Fray

The urges to maintain distance, to look inside for singular solutions to difficulties, and to confront anxieties as unemotionally as possible retain their magnetic strength for the avoidant. At the beginning of the fourth session with Vincent and Elizabeth, for example, the one in which he announced that maybe they could do without so much counseling after all, we arrived a few minutes late for our appointed meeting. We found Vincent sitting in a chair reading his *Wall Street Journal* and Elizabeth on the couch across the room balancing her checkbook. No conversation or behaviors between them gave any indication of the reasons they had come. They were out of the fray.

Like most avoidants, your wish to withdraw from any discussion that feels messy or threatens to get heated is probably great. Stick it out. Remind yourself: "It's not good for me to pull back. I need to talk."

Nate has become pretty good about sticking it out. He remembers, when all his job troubles were peaking, how Elena sometimes asked what was going on, and how he either calmly or angrily put her off. He didn't want to talk about it. (Elena, of course, also wishing to avoid the reality that some big trouble was afoot and, especially, to escape a conflictual conversation with her partner, herself then quickly backed off from the confrontation.) Now, when he and Elena start talking about an uncomfortable issue, he gives himself an instruction. "I tell myself to keep my seat. My tendency is to retreat, physically—just get up and walk away. Go over to the computer. Now I don't so much, or if I do, I go back and sit down. Even if I can't think of anything I want to say to Elena, I go back."

Eliminate Sarcasm

Sarcasm is one of the avoidant's favorite weapons. Although it's unpleasant, a sarcastic put-down or comeuppance from your partner might start a mini-fight and that actually feels good, because it releases the sense of isolation.

Elizabeth described this phenomenon quite neatly in the example she gave of a recent small episode. Vincent had asked her to pick up a pair of new trousers he'd left to be cuffed at their tailor's and she forgot. When he realized that evening that she had not retrieved the pants, Elizabeth recounts: "Vincent said to me, 'Well, how was Mr. Stavic when you picked up my pants today? Business flourishing over there?' It really made me annoyed, the way he said that, and it started an argument. But at least when we have an argument, I feel there's some connection with him." This is actually a hopeful comment from her. She's right. At least they're getting something cooking between them.

Sarcastic behavior, however, is biting behavior, the use of the sword. It won't improve the connectedness over the long haul. Elizabeth might have replied to her husband's comment: "You're being sarcastic. I gather you're pretty angry right now." Although a flat-footed and perhaps artificial-sounding remark, that's nevertheless a clear statement of her accurate observation. An alternative: "You know, I'd like it better if you said, 'I guess you didn't get time to pick up my pants today, huh?' " Any such comment ideally will serve to take them both out of the biting mode for a while; if afterward they return to their respective huts, at least they are getting in a little practice at establishing a new pattern of expressing discontent.

You will always recognize a sarcastic response from your partner, but might not spot your own similar behavior. Agree that you will make a joint effort to eliminate these essentially nasty and evasive remarks.

Run a Joint Daily Anxiety Check

During one of our sessions, Pamela mentions an unpleasant bit of office politics that had left her feeling out of the loop recently on a significant case. After discussing the what-she-might-have-said, what-to-do-next alternatives, we ask if she's talked any of this over with Matt. "No," says Pamela, "we both have such long work days and such crazy schedules, when we get together or talk on the phone, I want to keep things pleasant."

"Keeping things pleasant" is certainly an appropriate aim, to a degree. As Pamela heads deeper into a long-term love relationship, she would do well to examine whether that tendency toward not voicing the disagreeable aspects of the day is an attempt to avoid seeking emotional support from her partner. She needs to get comfortable with anxiety checks.

Anxiety checks may feel contrived when you start, but try this. Each evening, briefly and simply tell each other about a person or incident that made you feel upset or angry during the day. Listen to each other with empathy but without necessarily posing solutions. The next day, follow up. Ask your partner if anything further happened in that matter; ask: "Is that stuff still on your mind, still bothering you?"

The goal here is to get in the habit of sharing emotions and the events that precipitated them, your personal small bad patches, and giving each other a few words of comfort, understanding, and support. It will feel good and bring you closer.

Get Over Being (or Living with) Mr. Nice Guy

There is nothing wrong with being a nice guy, of course, but more is called for between lovers. Avoidant partners— especially what we've called the "well-socialized" ones, the ones who don't want just to be left alone and snarl at all who would come close—find it easy to be accommodating. Genuine engagement is another matter.

Elena gives many examples of how "nice" her husband is because of the little pleasantries he performs for her. "If he gets up to get a soda, for example," she says, "he'll always ask me if I want one too. Things like that." Bringing her a soda or a cup of coffee is an action he is able to take, since it requires little of him; talking about feelings or involving her in the issues of his life (such as his job going down the drain) are actions he cannot take without experiencing discomfort, the possibility of a conflict, and the threat of being abandoned. And Elena latches on to those nice-guy behaviors when she's impelled by her own attachment style to continue to deny the true flavor of her relationship.

Vincent and Elizabeth, after many years of marriage, are living a joint life defined largely by accommodation. And there's much visible evidence that it's chugging along just fine. The kids *are* healthy and decent and doing well in school. Vincent *is* a good provider and comes home on time every night and is devoted to his family. And Elizabeth *is* an attentive wife and mother. They've got a great apartment and a vacation house as well. What's so bad?

So Elizabeth reverts regularly to telling herself she has few grounds for complaint against her "wonderful husband, wonderful father" partner. Her mother, who's noticed Elizabeth's blue moods, tells her the same—leave him alone, what more do you want? With all these proofs and internal and external voices coming at her, Elizabeth was able to act for a long time as if she didn't need the connection that simply had never grown between her and her husband. And she didn't need it, until recently.

Many accommodations add up to something less than a real partnership or a truly intimate connection. Besides, just because your partner is often nicely accommodating doesn't make him genuinely thoughtful or kind. This is a tough nut for any Mr. Nice Guy to swallow, sensitive as he or she is to criticism and eager to avoid being caught out as not such a saint after all.

The point is not to stop making the nice gestures toward your partner or accepting them from him or her. Nice gestures, after all, sweeten the day. The point is, don't interpret the obliging interactions as evidence that all is well. Nor should you be surprised at feelings of discontent that may surface in your mind and heart when you accept the nice gestures. They are, after all, an essentially surface form of intimacy, no more and no less than the polite behaviors we'd offer a stranger. Don't be hard on yourself for wanting more, in other words, and continue to strive for something infinitely more satisfying.

Don't Label

Reduce your tendency to make sweeping judgments of your partner or of anyone based on one bit of behavior.

Avoidants generally are most comfortable with absolutes, because absolutes relieve them of the human need to sort through a myriad of negative and positive feelings. Seeing others in one-dimensional terms, however, makes it virtually impossible to connect and to be empathetic.

Elizabeth found us by seeking the recommendation of her cousin, a woman who had been through a marital separation and reconciliation and was one of our clients. Although he was content to let his wife pick the therapist, and he appeared dutifully for our initial sessions, Vincent found a way right off the bat to devalue his partner's choice. As we talked in our first meeting about what brought them here and a bit about her cousin Lillian, Vincent said, in a jocular manner, "Liz and Lil, the ditz girls," and related an irrelevant story of some minor bungled arrangements the cousins had recently made.

Putting Elizabeth down as "a ditz" is a way Vincent can avoid counseling; he is suggesting that since it was initiated by such an unstable source he doesn't have to take it all terribly seriously. If he often applies that or similarly cute but disparaging labels to his partner, Elizabeth must fight against accepting his characterization of her. To accept it enables her to deny her strengths and assets, and to have an even harder time identifying herself as a competent woman, which indeed she is.

Consider your own tendency to label, and what it helps you to avoid. Perhaps it is easy for you to think, "He's a spendthrift . . . therefore we can never talk about a budget in any sane way . . . therefore I'll have to take care of it on my own." Avoidants love taking care of matters on their own; they feel that all the pieces exist somewhere in their heads and they can pull them together just like that, when necessary.

But all that self-reliance, and labeling of your partner, is a way of escaping emotional contact. It puts off interacting and gives permission to go down your own path. And as we've been saying, to make a better couple fit you want to get on the same path with more regularity.

CHAPTER 11

Cool in the Heart of a Storm:
The Avoidant/Ambivalent Couple

HE AND SHE

O<small>UR</small> couple sits down, looking more than a bit uncomfortable. He clutches our list, appears to study it with care, but nothing on it seems to get him going. After a quick glance, she takes the initiative.

SHE: Well, let's start with paying attention to finances. You know I have a charge at the market. When I was in there yesterday the manager handed me copies of the last two months' bills, which he said very diplomatically had probably got lost in the mail. It was embarrassing. You don't pay that bill because you don't like me shopping there.

HE: The most overpriced market in the neighborhood.

SHE: It's not overpriced. It's expensive because it has the best quality food.

(Silence.)

SHE: Well, do you have something else to say about that?

HE: I would say you pay much more attention to food than I do. I don't really care that much.

SHE: No, that's not so. You do care. You enjoy the meals I prepare and you expect them. Like last week, when I told you I was meeting Millie for dinner and you could make yourself a sandwich, you got a very pouty expression on your face.

So, this is not true, that you don't care. You're like your mother, who wants everybody to see her as good and wonderful and self-denying but who's really all wrapped up in herself. You like to think, "I'm just a simple guy, anything goes for me," but it's not true. You like the idea of having this little philosophy, that a real man doesn't worry a lot about basics. But you do care. And you should. It's important.

(Throughout her explanation of what's wrong with him, her partner has had a wan smile on his face. It will remain there for the rest of the session, as he continues to look distractedly at our little list in hand.)

HE: Lateness . . . I don't spend as much time getting ready as you do.

SHE: Oh, yes you do. You spend just as much time as I do.

HE: No, I don't.

SHE: How come you're always late then and I'm always on time when we're going out? Also, you go to the barber shop all the time. . . .

HE: Once a month, to get my hair cut.

SHE: Well, I hardly ever go to the hairdresser. If you compare me to my friends . . . you should see my friends, they're going for hair treatments, hot oil treatments, cuts, coloring, all the time, once a week at least. I don't do that.

(He adds nothing to this observation; she's run out of steam. After a few moments, he reads from the list.)

HE: "How do arguments start?" *(looking at the camera)* I think we just covered that one.

(Another pause. He consults his list again.)

HE: Showing appreciation . . . do you want to say anything?
SHE: Well, I'd like it if you'd show you appreciate me by giving me little gifts from time to time, bring me some flowers.
HE *(in a barely discernible voice)*: I don't feel I can please you.
SHE: I know, that's why I don't take this as a personal rejection anymore.
HE *(more sighs)*: I wish you wouldn't be so tense and demanding about it.
SHE: I have no idea what you mean. If I knew what you meant, I'd try not to do that anymore.
HE: Nothing I buy on my own pleases you. I've learned not to try.
SHE: How many ways are there that I can say I like something? Maybe you're interpreting something as displeased or demanding when it's not really demanding at all.

(Silence.)

HE *(reading)*: Expressing emotions.
SHE: Expressing emotions. You don't express yourself at all. No one is allowed to know what you're think-

ing. I'm not even supposed to know what you're thinking about the co-op board vote, although that is something that affects me too.

(The therapist comes in to announce that ten minutes are up. Later, the reconciliation.)

SHE *(leg jumping, hands jittering)*: So, what should we talk about? Well, what are you going to do today? Did you pick up those tickets yet?

HE: I didn't get around to it.

SHE: If you don't get around to it pretty soon, there won't be any point.

HE: I am going to do it.

(Silence. He's perusing his list again.)

SHE: So . . . argue with me.

HE: I don't like arguing with you.

SHE: Why? Because I always win?

HE: No, I just find it very unpleasant.

SHE: No, it's because you can't take the confrontation.

(He looks over at her with a small smile.)

SHE *(laughing)*: What? Why are you looking at me with that standoff air?

HE: It's that I dislike your enthusiasm for the confrontation.

SHE *(more laughing)*: I don't believe it! It depends. There are arguments and there are arguments. When the argument is serious, I don't like the confrontation. When it's not so serious, like buying the tickets, then I do like to argue. But in general, I really don't like arguing. I don't know why you would say that.

HE *(looking at the camera)*: That's kind of hard to prove from this conversation we've been having.

SHE: Why don't you argue with me once in a while, tell me what I'm doing wrong?

HE: I get no pleasure out of that.

(Five minutes are up . . . the bell sounds.)

In this husband we see a classic example of the unadorned avoidant. He starts out motionless and remains so, somewhat sunk into his chair, holding on to our list for dear life throughout the ten minutes and almost never raising his eyes from it. Staring at that piece of paper is clearly more comfortable than looking at his wife.

On the other hand, she is a study in perpetual motion. She swings her foot, plays with her glasses, or twiddles a lock of hair. Her eyes dart up, down, and everywhere, often at her husband.

Being on the defensive is our avoidant husband's M.O.—like a prizefighter on the losing end of a battle, he keeps his gloved fists firmly in front of his face as his partner jabs away. And jab she does, picking a fight right off the bat. Watching her on the tape, we wonder if she wishes she had a hat pin handy, so she could give him a poke every so often.

He clearly understands what she means about keeping her in the dark regarding some business relating to their apartment. He avoids the content, however; he is not about to explore the matter again, or apologize, or try to explain himself.

This fellow pretty much evades every topic his partner brings up, right from the start, and never carries the discussion along. Meanwhile, she's working hard at getting a little conflict going, never stepping far outside her ambivalent's fighting mode—she picks, accuses, and puts him down. When she does produce a reaction, she pounces, which, of course, has the effect of driving him back into his lair. One hears an almost plaintive desperation in her last effort to stir up her nonreacting mate—argue with me once in a while, tell me what I'm doing wrong . . . please!

DAVID AND CAROLINE

David's a creative director in a large advertising firm, and looks the part—a natty dresser in a pale tan suit, navy shirt, and peacock blue tie, with an excellent haircut. Caroline works as a coordinator for a fashion designer, lining up model shoots and so on. They have lived together for five years in a relationship that clearly survives at least in part on some very satisfactory sex and on her need for someone to keep her life running on a fairly reasonable keel, a role David is willing to fill.

"If it wasn't for him, I'd probably starve to death," she says. David cooks the meals, pays the bills, and gets her up and out in the morning. And she's appreciative—mostly. Other times, her partner's supportive actions irk her. One evening last week, Caroline relates, her mother called; instead of waking Caroline from her nap to come to the phone, David chatted pleasantly with her mother for a while and said he'd have Caroline call back the next day. Later, Caroline was enraged: "He takes it upon himself to decide when I should or should not talk to my mother. And then he gets smarmy with her so she thinks he's God's gift to women."

David replies that Caroline has a difficult relationship with her mother, and that just the night before when the phone rang, Caroline said, "If that's my mother, tell her I'm out."

Volatile, ambivalent Caroline pumps the noise into this twosome; she's always emoting, always stirring up the pot. Meanwhile, David avoids absorbing the full *Sturm und*

Drang of Caroline's emotions by being "in charge" and keeping life humming along. He has a good, calming effect on her—when she is off on some tangential rant, he'll hear her out for a while, then say, "Well, what's your point?" and encourage her to simmer down and focus. She might roll her eyes at him and be annoyed, as she often is. At some level, though, she understands that most men would have a tough time dealing with her. In fact, she has never before sustained a relationship for as long as she's been with David.

The significance of the in-charge role he plays vis-à-vis Caroline and her mother, too, is critical to Caroline's functioning and cannot be overemphasized. Caroline suffered abuse as a child from an older half-brother, and she does rely on David to help keep her afloat in the painful atmosphere that characterizes her complicated family relationships and many friendships.

David does, however, have a temper. Lately, he has been storming off to spend a few nights at a friend's apartment. They both have a sense that something's coming to a head, and decided to try to talk it out with a therapist.

LARRY AND RACHEL

Larry and Rachel became engaged in college and married during graduate school. Then he completed his MBA and joined an investment firm while she quit her journalism job to stay home with their twins. Eleven years into the marriage, Rachel came to therapy because of feelings of depression. She was down a lot of the time, she said, "for no very obvious reason," but was aware that she switched between feeling pumped up and energized or low and listless. Over the previous half year the low and listless moods seemed to be prevailing. During one of the lows, she impulsively had a brief affair with an old friend. "I just saw him a couple of times, then broke it off," she says. But it scared her. Larry is also feeling a little scared because he knows something's bothering his wife. He wishes she were in a generally cheerier mood, so he has agreed to submit to counseling.

Larry would appear to be a prime example of the cool, critical, passive-aggressive avoidant who comes across in some ways as a real sweetie. A low-key man, he's slow to anger and slow to blame; their friends think he's a great guy. Rachel liked all that about him from the start; when they were first seeing each other as twenty-year-olds, she thought, " 'Here's somebody with a really good, easygoing disposition, good manners.' He wasn't like the other guys I knew." For Larry back then, "she was very strong, clear-minded about people."

Besides, Larry is responsible and reliable in his business affairs, and she admires that. He is deeply involved in community activities; he is a deacon in their church and he sits on several boards. She admired that, too—for a while. They're also both mentally quick and big readers; they've always found each other intellectually stimulating.

Now, it seems, Rachel has a lot of grievances to get off her chest. Larry is out every other night at one of his organizations, so he doesn't have dinner with the family very often and he doesn't take care of their two cars. He threw a hissy fit the other month over the cost of an all-out party for their kids' tenth birthday, although during all the preparations he'd said nothing and let her carry on. He's been telling her for two years that she would probably be happy having some kind of work outside the house, but now that she's taken a part-time job as a researcher, he complains. They spend too much time with his parents, whom she finds intrusive and irritating.

Rachel displays a lot of sadness too, especially over the

death of her father a year earlier: "My mom was a total maniac when I was growing up. I never knew what to expect from her, but my father was a rock." She becomes teary as she talks about her dad, but when Larry reaches over in a gesture of comfort, she glares and yanks her hand away—an action that seems to express the idea, Now you're finally waking up?

KENT AND JEANETTE

A professional couple, these two have been married for twenty-two years. In most areas, avoidant Jeanette and ambivalent Kent are a good match, in the mutually dependent manner of many avoidant/ambivalent twosomes.

He's an executive vice-president of a large newspaper chain. She has a government job.

Both are successful at what they do for a living and they help each other out in their professional lives. His involves a fair amount of entertaining, and Jeanette, an engagingly social woman who clearly loves keeping very, very busy, has no problem arranging the dinner and cocktail parties and overseeing all house details, in addition to keeping track of their two kids. She's happy to take charge of all that, and most of the time doesn't mind his harping around with frequent, small where's-the-butter? type complaints.

Although she's excellent at her work, her duties there often stir up Jeanette's anxieties, especially when she's facing a troublesome situation that promises to involve some conflict or differences between herself and a colleague. When she needs to sway a course of action and press for her point of view, she almost always turns to Kent for advice, and he's good at giving it.

He loves conflict and confrontation. In fact, he's always

searching for a little conflict, sniffing it out constantly, nip-
ping at the smallest speck. He's ready at the drop of a hat
to overwhelm another with his argument. Hammering away
is his passion, while hers is to remain conflict-free and protected. So when she's getting nervous about a presentation
she must make or some other work situation, she pulls him
in, discusses the problem at length, and takes in from him
some of that energy and passion. She uses his ability to fight
to fortify herself and become more capable at what's required of her.

A patient partner, Jeanette tries hard to keep her husband
quiet by giving him what he wants. Occasionally, she will
have a small blowup over all the demands. Then her annoyance hypes his anger, she gets scared, and she rushes to reconnect. And he's always willing to reconnect, which usually
happens over sex.

It works. The children, however, apparently create much
conflict for these two, especially now that their daughter,
Lindy, and son, Ian, are full-fledged teenagers. Neither child
is turning out to be either parent's idea of a pride and joy.
Both high achievers themselves, Kent and Jeanette express
their disappointment and puzzlement over the fact that their
kids are, at best, indifferent students. Seventeen-year-old
Lindy recently announced that she has no intention of scout-
ing colleges and plans instead to roam across the country
with some friends after graduation, picking up odd jobs as
needed. Thirteen-year-old Ian not only brings home poor
grades, but has dropped his previous interest in soccer and
karate.

Jeanette has preferred not to think much about any of this,
believing that her children are "going through growing
phases." Kent, on the other hand, describes himself as "furious at these kids. They're lazy. They don't want to put in
the work." She avoids and denies; he's mad as hell that his

children are causing him problems. Their differing but equally unproductive reactions have almost surely contributed to the confusion their children seem to be experiencing.

Lately, Jeanette and Kent have been starting to sit up and take closer notice. Jeanette, especially, was shaken by the possibility that Ian isn't simply working out some growing pains, but is in danger of slipping through the cracks. After a teacher suggested Ian was in fairly desperate need of outside tutoring if he was to keep up with his class, Jeanette sought some professional counseling for the boy and then for herself and her husband. This was no small accomplishment, because Kent put up an argument about "goddamn therapy" for several months, and she backed down a few times before finally persevering.

In its starkest forms, the ambivalent/avoidant relationship can be a heartbreaker, consisting of one desperately needy individual continually rebuffed by a chronically and coldly withholding partner. Consider the heroine of Tolstoy's famous novel, *Anna Karenina*, a woman of excessive passions married to Karenin, a classic avoidant, who pats his wife on the head condescendingly, believing that to be an adequate display of understanding and closeness. Vulnerable to crushes, dissatisfied in a marriage that is not intense enough for her, Anna falls for Vronsky and takes him as her lover. He's a charming fellow with social skills, but another avoidant who must dodge the reality of any difficult relationship. Poor Anna—in nineteenth-century Russia, an adulteress pregnant with Vronsky's illegitimate child—is jealous, miserable, moody, and eventually suicidal.

In its less melodramatic displays, the avoidant/ambivalent pair can be puzzling. Can you see from our several couple stories how the relationship often might have a good-cop/bad-cop look to it, from the outside? We'd guess their friends and relatives probably see avoidant David, Larry, and Jeanette as the good guys here, the rock on which the couple survives. Each is perceived as the one who's steady, agreeable, and clear. Friends also probably think of ambivalent Caroline, Rachel, and Kent as problematic—needy, irrational, critical, demanding, or angry and ready to pick a fight.

The inside story of such pairs often reads somewhat differently. True, the avoidant hates argument and conflict, but he may get mad, store it up, and then erupt. Possibly, like David, he must remove himself from the scene at regular intervals if he is to maintain a grip on his own equilibrium. The ambivalent, who so often seems out of control, is the one who at least does respond, in one way or another, to the emotional underpinnings of their joint life.

But these two *can* make each other feel whole.

The ambivalent looks to her calm and steady mate for reining in, to keep her own seesawing emotions contained. Caroline would "starve to death," she's sure, without her lover, or be buried by that mother. Her partner is "laid back," says Rachel, "while I always tend to fly off the handle."

The avoidant may be grateful to and enjoy his partner for all that energy issuing forth, and for allowing feelings to be expressed, something he's loath to do. Often, the more volatile partner is perceived as wonderfully sensitive and intuitive about the world. "Rachel," Larry says, "tunes in to people; she picks up on what's going on."

At the same time, the minuses in this pair can be significant. As long as ambivalents like Caroline and Rachel keep trying to satisfy their strong dependency needs and requests for constant reassurance through their partners, they're not doing what they must do to develop a truly internal sense of self. Even powerfully blustery ambivalents, like Kent, who's determined to carry the day in any disagreement, are depending excessively on the partner's response in order to feel strong. And as long as the avoidant feels solely responsible for keeping life humming along, he's in danger of turning into a control freak.

In fact, true engagement between any of our couples is difficult. This pair may forget entirely what issues they really ought to settle. Since the ambivalent is overwhelmed by emotions and the avoidant has a hard time expressing them, there's an air of unreality to their interactions.

Arguments tend to go nowhere. While the ambivalent gets more intense and angry and goes on the attack, the avoidant becomes more rigid and defensive. Afterward, life continues as before until the next frustrating attempt to engage, and then more steam is let off.

TOWARD A MORE COMFORTABLE COUPLE FIT

FOR THE AMBIVALENT

Bite Your Tongue

In the course of a counseling session with this pair, there often comes a point at which the ambivalent partner takes the attack right over the top and goes for the jugular, saying things like, "You really are a total jerk! You're just like your father—he never knew what he was talking about either, which is probably why he got Alzheimer's." Those zingers are not only hurtful and beside the point, but they also obviously pump up the animosity level and tend to stop any purposeful conversation in its tracks. We might suggest that some good homework for this couple is to avoid the jugular and practice a little biting of the tongue.

Kent, for example, is an angry, in-your-face ambivalent;

Jeanette is a not-especially withdrawn or chilly avoidant. So these two do routinely mix it up; conflicts and arguments particularly get cooking, as we've noted, over issues regarding their two children. Although they know this is an area in which they must pull together, especially now when both their daughter and their son could use real guidance, they have not been working that way.

Kent loves his kids, but he can't just settle down and be a good guy. He switches on and off, from acting in an understanding way to sounding like a punitive, nasty, attacking father (just like the father he had). "On occasion he's called Lindy 'a bum,' " says Jeanette. "He's called Ian 'a wimp.' " Kent sheepishly acknowledges that has been the case. Jeanette gets mad, the kids get upset, and a lot of acting out takes place. Kent feels bad about his nasty words, and reverts to his good-guy mode, for a while. With little consistency in his approaches to them, the children don't know what to expect from him, except his frequent anger.

The truth of the matter is—although perhaps he doesn't realize it and might not admit it if he did—Kent really wants both kids at a distance, out of the house. It is possible that Jeanette wouldn't mind that development either. With the conflict factors (two children) out of the picture, this couple could more comfortably maintain their respective attachment styles within their mutually dependent intimate relationship. But the kids *are* in their lives, and are going to be for some time, and at least one of them needs supportive help.

The nastiness hurts the whole family now, and poisons any efforts to come to some sensible decisions. Biting his tongue will be hard for Kent, but it behooves him to make the attempt. And his wife can help him along. Try to pull the plug on an argument before he loses it, we suggest. She knows this man well enough to spot the signs and signals that he's working up a head of steam, and she can deflect the squall before it reaches gale force. She can say: "This discussion is about to degenerate into name-calling, and I don't want that. I don't think you do either. So let's stop now, and talk later with cooler heads."

If your avoidant partner is of the calm, remote, Great Stone Face variety, it's probably easy for you to go too far when you're trying to get a reaction. And Lord knows, he or she has the capacity to push you right up and over the top. Try very hard to quell your urge to voice your discontent with low blows or irrelevant and hurtful observations.

Don't Rush to Fill Every Silence

Another aspect to biting your tongue.

Even when not motivated to indulge in low blows or hurtful observations, the ambivalent partner in this duo often tends to keep talking—a lot. Look back at our He and She dialogue, and see how she can't seem to sit still and keep quiet. Silence, expressive as it is of her mate's distance, offends her. We wonder what might happen if she paused to take a deep breath now and then, and looked at him with a small, friendly smile, and just let the silence linger a bit? Although we can surely be sympathetic to her wish for greater responsiveness on his part, it's easy to speculate also that her doing his talking for him isn't bringing that wish closer to fulfillment.

Doing all the talking perpetuates aspects of the pas de deux between you and your partner that you should hope to renegotiate. This allows him, indeed encourages him, to keep his distance and retreat to his hut; you, possibly, keep fanning the flames of your own annoyance over doing all the work. Even more critically, you diminish the likelihood of his developing certain useful skills, such as the ability to express his own needs clearly.

Here's an example: Caroline and her lover do a fair amount of socializing with friends, and these are usually enjoyable evenings, she says, "except that sometimes the conversations get noisy and animated, and David starts feeling left out. I'll know he wants to be on stage and get into the action when he kind of moves to the edge of his chair and tries to catch my eye. He can't just jump in on his own—he signals me to help him and bring him in."

Sometimes she does. Sometimes she doesn't. "He looks so needy and dependent," she says. "Occasionally, I find this kind of cute and I help him out. Other times, it absolutely infuriates me—it's like I'm supposed to save him. If I'm involved myself in what's going on, then I just ignore him."

For his part, David is apparently only dimly aware of his behavior and how it prompts those he's-so-cute or I-want-to-kill-him reactions: "I don't think I'm 'needy,' " he says, "it's just that she's so lively and juiced and talkative when we go out. I'm not such a party animal."

We'd guess that David has become so accustomed to Caroline's doing all the talking and making up for his silences in their relationship that he relies on that dynamic to carry him through some uncomfortable social patches, where he'd *like* to be a bit more of a party animal but doesn't know how. On Caroline's behalf, we can say she is, at least, responsive to her partner. But her inconsistent maybe-I-will, maybe-I-won't-help-you-out reactions effectively keep both enmeshed in an old pattern that calls for readjustment. Since she is often "infuriated" by his need, as she sees it, to be bailed out in those social situations, she'd do well to try to talk this out a bit with her partner.

"Suppose you explained your feelings to David," we suggest, "but not right after the party's over and you're in a mood either to love or to hate his neediness. In a more neutral moment or before the next evening out, tell him you'd like it if he tried harder to keep engaged with the goings-on and not look to you so much." She thinks she could do that; he thinks he could try harder.

Helping each other renegotiate the fit involves helping each other become more of a "self-feeder," as we've called it. Maintaining a bit more silence—not a fuming, hostile silence, but a relaxed, affectionate, understanding silence—may give your avoidant partner a push toward shoring up his own self-confidence and powers of expression. Staying quieter and pausing more frequently might be difficult for you at first, but "fewer words better chosen" is a good way to get your partner to open up and to improve communication between the two of you.

Stick to the Issues

Caroline hates it when David takes his mini-breaks to spend a night or two at his friend's place: "I'll know he's really mad about something when he leaves in the morning, and then I am just waiting for him to call me during the day and say he thinks he's going to see Vinnie after work and I shouldn't wait up for him." She's desperate for him to return, and after David cools off, he does return, to a usually passionate reconciliation. Soon—and it may be really soon, within an hour or two—she's pushing him away again.

David relates this incident: "I've had a habit for years of tossing all my small change in a jar at the end of the day, and then at some point I take it out and get it counted and put it in the bank. This is some prehistoric holdover from when I was a kid and we used to roll up our pennies and dimes all year and use the money to buy Christmas presents." Caroline has indicated several times that the sight of this jar of coins on their bedroom window sill offends her. On this particular evening, not long after the getting back together and the sexy making up, "she suddenly started grousing about this jar," says David, "how it was so disgusting and dirty and she was going to get rid of it. This is out of the blue."

David, of course, may have his issues percolating about the jar of coins—how come he *hasn't* put it out of sight? But of primary importance in that evening's mise-en-scène was Caroline's inability to stick to the occurrence that had so upset her, and her need to get right back into fighting mode. Once she and her lover had reconnected, it was business as usual, with the issue unaddressed. We suggest: "It seems you and David need to do some talking about his 'running off,' as you say, which upsets you a lot. You're both going to be in a better mood to start doing that if you're not having a fight. So when the jar of coins or another grievance flares up in your mind, decide you'll come back to that one at some future date, and give both of you more time to feel comfortable."

In the relative calm of our office session, Caroline gets the point and agrees that's an excellent idea. In the comparative hurly-burly of one of those bedroom scenes, however, she'll have to work a lot harder to keep herself sticking to the issue. What she really needs and wants to say to David is something like this: "I don't feel loved, because when you become angry and upset with me, you leave me. You're not here. I'd feel so much better if you'd stay, and try to talk to me, and help me understand what's making you angry." But to speak of those deeper feelings of abandonment and loss is terribly uncomfortable, and so what comes out instead is: "I have to look at that jar of coins all the time! You don't love me!" To complain about the coins is effectively to divert energy away from altering the attachment style toward a better fit.

As you think about sticking to the issue at hand in your relationship, make it one complaint—or let's call it one correction—at a time. If you have insisted that your partner come home to join the family for dinner, don't start needling him about how he never takes the car for servicing once he's at the dinner table. Squelch your tendency to revert back to fighting mode.

Identifying small, habitual behaviors from your partner that bug you is a helpful step in learning to stick to the issue. Most of the couples we counsel don't have a lot of trouble with this assignment—it takes him a good half hour to feel in the mood to say more than "Hi" when he comes home every evening and I want to talk; she loses things and has me constantly trolling around to find her reading glasses.

Think about your own list. Write it down. Ponder it. Are these matters important? Do you love your partner anyway? Can you let some of these matters go?

Get in the Habit of Asking Yourself, "Can This Wait?"

Caroline spends money impulsively, a tendency that bothers her partner. "It's not because we're hard up," says David, "or that I begrudge her treating herself. But she always seems to have to confess to me about it. It gets annoying."

As they talk about this issue, it seems apparent that his annoyance does not have to do with the spent money or even with the confession, but with some bad timing on his lover's part. Recently, for example, Caroline got a $350 hair coloring job, then rushed straight from the salon to a phone to call David at work and "apologize" for her extravagance. She needed to get the matter off her chest at once. "He acted cold and hung up in a hurry," she says, and she figured he was angry at her. If she had contained herself, we ask, and waited until they were together at home that evening to discuss her pricey head of hair, would things have gone better? Yes, they probably would have, she thinks.

A healthy habit any ambivalent living with an avoidant should develop is to ask yourself, "Can this wait?" A little containment and better timing may work wonders in reducing the intensity of your avoidant partner's reaction—his tendency to become cool, withdrawn, or critical when confronted with an emotional issue that's on your mind.

Try (Hard) Not to Have to Be Right All the Time

Or to repeatedly justify your behavior (because then you can calm down), or to keep at your avoidant partner until he admits he's wrong and says he's sorry or in some way or other gives in. He may *be* wrong and you may *get* your apology, but it will be a hollow victory. He will sometimes apologize as a way of stopping the spat, but he isn't, in fact, terribly sorry at all, and ends up resentful and even more likely to display the sarcastic or withdrawn behaviors by which he shows he's peeved.

That's a lesson Rachel started to learn as she rehashed, during one of our sessions, her anger over Larry's birthday party hissy fit. "He exploded at me over the money I spent," she says, "although I had told him about the plans I was making several times and he didn't care." She turns to her partner: "Admit it. Isn't that true? You didn't give a damn, and then afterward you get on your high horse and act like you're so responsible and I'm so irresponsible and can't be trusted to know what I'm doing." He says he guesses so. "No, it's not just you *guess so*," she comes right back at him, "you made things very unpleasant that evening for me and the boys, and it wasn't fair." He says he's sorry.

So Rachel gets her apology and simmers down; however, a loaded, hostile silence ensues. "What would be a good way to handle the next issue that comes up about household expenses?" we wonder aloud. Could she try a little harder to pull him in and he try a little harder to pay attention to mundane activities? They talk about this a bit and see some paths to improvement.

Ideally, Rachel takes away the idea that being right or on the side of "what's fair" isn't always so important if she hopes to work out a more comfortable couple fit. She can help him become more involved with the partnership, to be a better colleague with her.

Try (Hard) Not to Keep Hammering Away Until You Get What You Want

Hammering away is a means by which the ambivalent partner gets affirmation, builds herself up. It goes deep into her identity; she views herself as not very powerful. If she can influence events to get what she wants, she's not helpless after all.

Hammering away can also be the ambivalent's response to the avoidant's aggravating behavior. Rachel saw this pretty clearly: "If I get ticked off about something, like we're supposed to meet friends at the theater and they're late, Larry is all, 'What's the big deal? Relax.' " That kind of typically avoidant response often drove her up the wall, bringing out the worst in her style and leading her to attack him. But she knew the fights were distracting to the family, and more and more, she had been withdrawing to keep the peace—and getting into those low and listless moods instead.

If she gets better at biting her tongue, sticking to the issue, and not needing to be right, she may reach a more comfortable ground, defined by neither angry outbursts nor depressed withdrawals. Any ambivalent living with an avoidant needs to understand this, however: You will never get all that you want from your partner, but that is not a sign that he doesn't care.

Become a Better Self-Feeder

The ambivalent finds it difficult to settle into the moment, to draw from the activity or the experience itself a full sense of satisfaction. Her feelings of comfort, accomplishment, self-esteem, personal power, or involvement are always tied in first and foremost to the other—to getting her partner to do what she wants, or to agree or disagree, or to offer approval or disapproval.

Shifting to a more internal satisfaction is what we call self-feeding.

FOR THE AVOIDANT

Be the Initiator; Don't Dodge the Challenges

As long as they've been married, Rachel has nagged Larry to keep her better informed about his schedule. Although it is a reasonable request, Larry almost always fails to give her advance notice about certain blips on the screen—a Saturday meeting he'll have to attend, and so on. Periodically, Rachel blows up over this issue, and then, she says, "He'll say something like, 'Well, how many days in advance do you want to know?' or 'Do you want this written down?' Dumb questions. Why doesn't he just do this simple thing?"

Larry waits until he has incurred his partner's anger, then attempts to pacify her by negotiating a little timetable. How much pleasanter this bit of life would be if Larry made an effort to overcome his avoidant's tendency to maintain his distance and simply volunteered, ahead of time, to keep Rachel up to speed about his schedule and appointments.

Withholding, letting the more expressive partner start things, seems to the avoidant what he must do or be to keep the peace. He can feel like the mature one, the container, but that's not quite the full story.

These twosomes allow the ambivalent to do all the confrontational acting out. By tolerating this emotional tug-of-war, the avoidant encourages it to continue. It actually feels comfortable to him—he's able to satisfy his need for involvement without having to initiate things or take chances; he merely must react.

Look back at our He and She couple at the start of this section. We might say that his response, "I don't feel I can please you," is a metaphor for his non-engagement with his partner and an excuse for his failure to initiate. The less he talks, acts, and asks for, the more noisy, frustrated, and demanding she becomes. The more she argues, the more he withholds. There's an avoidant power play at work here, and, of course, neither is able to understand the other's position.

Being the initiator a lot more frequently than you are now means you're going to have to talk more. Before you can do that, you may need to find your own rigorously honest answer to this question: Am I secretly enjoying the sense of power I get from stirring up all those intense emotions in my lover?

Stop Being So Agreeable

You tend to be overly accommodating, in an effort to settle down your overreacting partner. But we can paint another, darker side to all the agreeable, accommodating nice-guy behavior. It is not always especially agreeable or nice at all, but rather, an effort to avoid conflict at all costs and to escape the anxiety of expressing wishes.

Kent brings up an incident that occurred when the family went out to a favorite Chinese restaurant for dinner, where they were in the habit of ordering several dishes to share. He asked his wife what she wanted, and Jeanette replied: "Whatever everybody wants is fine by me." She then turned to their son Ian and said, "You like the shrimp in garlic sauce, don't you?" He did indeed, and said he'd order that.

Whereupon Kent got mad. "You know I can't stand shrimp, we've been through this before," he said. Father and son began to argue, and Ian said he didn't feel like dinner anyway. This is a man with a lot of free-floating anger in general. Remember that it's important to him that he get his way, because that makes him feel better about himself. So it was easy to picture this spat over the shrimp.

What did Jeanette have to say while it was going on? Apparently, nothing. "No, that's not true," says Kent now, "you said, 'I don't know why you two guys can't get along better.' "

Here's an avoidant pattern revealed. Mom sets up her son (whom she loves dearly) to express her wishes (she also loves shrimp and garlic) and uses him as a shield against her husband. She pushes the battle elsewhere, lets Ian do the dirty work and request the dreaded shrimp, forcing him to deal with Dad's annoyance. She sits back, no participant in the scene at all, looking puzzled, and thinks, gee, what's wrong with you two?

Here's how she might better handle the scene and get some practice in overcoming her avoidant/agreeable tendencies. When Kent asks, "What do you want?" he isn't actually seeking an answer to that question—he is, in fact, being a bit magnanimous, allowing her a say, which he will then protest. She is aware of all this, in fact, so she needs to be able to say something along these lines: "Are you really asking me what I want? You know what I always like when we come here. And you know when I tell you what I want you're going to argue about it. Now, I think we don't have to make such a production about this. For another $10.95 you can order an extra dish, and I'll have my shrimp, and you don't have to eat it."

Behind every avoidant's accommodating agreeableness lurks a deep-seated fear of abandonment, perhaps even annihilation from the ambivalent's rage. The avoidant's passion attaches to that need to keep things always on an even keel, even at the expense of pushing the battle onto the child. Arguing, fighting, even expressing one's wishes produce great anxiety, because the fight stirs the fear. (Jeanette would also do well to remind herself that, after twenty-two years of a basically solid marriage, it's unlikely that anybody's going to be abandoning anybody.)

Ponder your own tendency toward an excess of agreeableness, all that giving in. When your mate is getting too aggressive, hold fast and express your needs.

Become More Self-Protective; Draw Your Line in the Sand

At a glance, it would appear our avoidant does a fine job of self-protection, in her cool, distant, keeping-out-the-fray style. But when she gives in repeatedly to the ambivalent's give-me-what-I-want demands, or seethes mightily but says nothing about the partner's fractious behavior, it's a denial of self.

Avoidants in this attachment-style twosome have to learn when and where to draw some lines in the sand.

David has become so good at knowing what Caroline wants, for example, that he will act on her wishes even before she gives voice to them—he rides a perpetual anticipating-and-doing merry-go-round. At the same time, secretly he gets pretty sick of all that accommodating and giving in. While the "I'll jump up and make coffee even before you ask" action is going on, another voice inside says, "In fact, I really just want to sit here and read the paper." And if David becomes aware of that fact, he can come to understand that his periodic furies and storming off to bunk elsewhere for a couple of days have much to do with being fed up at all the anticipating and doing.

But he can't just come right out and speak up; he can't say, "You know, I just don't want to do six more things tonight, and run interference for you with your mother and your girlfriend. I need to relax and goof off and I'm feeling a little put-upon here." It's the abandonment issue surfacing in avoidant style—If I stand up for myself, speak my piece, and say what I want, my partner will abandon me, so I'll keep quiet and wait for my partner to protect me by *not* expecting me to take on the six more things. And of course the ambivalent partner isn't likely to come around and do that.

By not saying what needs to be said to attain a measure of self-protection, David is, in fact, abandoning himself. If it goes on and becomes a deeply ingrained habit of interaction, there's a terrible diminishing of the self.

Extreme examples of that loss of identity seem to occur most frequently in women, in particular the homemaker avoidant woman attached to the aggressive, demanding, ambivalent man. In practice, we've seen her often over the years. Usually, she comes for counseling after the fact, when the marriage or relationship has finally crashed. It's difficult to know, then, how she started out, but crystal clear that she has become something of an empty shell—whatever once was there is now so depleted that only the most fragile element of self-esteem remains.

For this homemaker wife who has derived little buoying up from outside accomplishments, the marriage is all; her self-image is relayed from the partner, the "caretaker." More than self-image—the caretaker throws out her only lifeline. But if the avoidant woman *presents* herself as she truly is, she fears she will be abandoned; she'll die. Occasionally that deep sense of potential abandonment reveals itself in a somatic manner—she becomes sick easily, has a sensitive stomach and can eat only certain foods, and so on. She does know what she thinks and feels, but from childhood on she's been powerfully discouraged from any expressions of the same.

Although she's far removed from the image of the empty-shell homemaker, Jeanette describes experiences from her earliest years with her parents, a depressive, sickly father and an anxious mother, that reveal how inexorably the avoidant style develops. Mom would frequently warn her daughter, "You'll kill your father," if you tell him that or do this or go there. If young Jeanette fell and badly scraped her knee, her mother might say, "For heaven's sake, stop crying, and whatever you do don't go whining to your father." Even physical pain was to be denied. It is not so surprising, then, that denial is often her grown-up resort—I don't know what I think and feel—in order to stay safe, to not be abandoned.

Of course, it doesn't work. Any time you can't depend on being loved for you, you will lose.

Becoming more self-protective, setting limits, and drawing lines in the sand speak to the avoidant's need to develop a stronger ability to contain his partner, who does need containment. The avoidant must learn to say: This is as far as I go. This I will put up with; that, I will not.

Here is an example: Larry sensed that his parents depended on him increasingly for a large measure of emotional support and comfort. He had been distant from them through much of his life, and now had a wish to reconnect, as they were aging and becoming vulnerable and somewhat frightened about life. He felt he could spend time with them now, and perhaps draw closer. He did not, as he saw it, impose his parents on Rachel to an excessive degree.

"But she's always in a foul mood before, during, and after any visit," he says. "She makes the day unpleasant. She makes little effort to be just basically polite to them sometimes."

"I'm sorry," says Rachel, "but I find your parents a pain in the ass."

Quite possibly, Rachel, in her ambivalent way, feels vaguely threatened by her partner's efforts to forge better emotional ties with his family. Regardless of what lies at the heart of her behavior toward them, Larry has allowed her moods to prevail most of the time, by canceling visits, cutting them short, or going alone. A bad rupture seems likely to happen over this matter of his family ties.

Larry would do well to learn to handle the issue in a more secure manner, which will involve drawing one of those lines in the sand and standing up to his partner. For example, he might say: "Look, you're right, my parents can be a pain in the ass sometimes. We don't have to go there every week or even every three weeks, but I like having you with me. They do like to see us together, they are my parents, and we're going to be polite and cut out the rude stuff, because that's just not acceptable to me. You say they're too intrusive. If there's something particular they're doing that's bothering you, tell me and I'll try to explain the situation to them. But I expect both of us to work at getting along with them."

He's telling his partner he's on her side by acknowledging her point, but the visits will continue and he won't tolerate the rudeness and unpleasantness. He's telling her he'll try harder to keep his parents in line, but he's going to keep her in line too.

Act on Your Instincts

This is another way of saying you should become more self-protective, relying more on your own feelings and less on all that input from your partner. And the avoidant, as we've said before, is really pretty good at feelings, intuitions, and instincts. He runs the risk, however, of allowing the ambivalent partner to call the shots, and of not recognizing sometimes that the called shots aren't really on target.

Avoidant Jeanette, for example, values her partner's sound advice and pumping up when she faces a troublesome job situation. She appreciates his smarts and insights and draws both ideas and strengths from them; he's good at the job-related advice and pumping up (he'll never offer her a general, for-no-particular-reason-pump-up, but at the specifics he shines). Moreover, he loves to give to her in this way and feel great about himself.

However, there is other advice he's all too willing to offer, that isn't particularly useful or even right. Jeanette has learned the hard way that she can't always accept her mate's judgments about other people—what they intend and how they should be treated. Because he's such a belligerent guy, so ready to call somebody "a horse's ass," for example, he's created a few real difficulties over the years. He takes stronger stands than are necessary, makes others angry, and shoots himself in the foot with some regularity. On occasion, Jeanette has realized ruefully that her partner, by behaving in his short-fuse manner, has made himself look foolish, and pulled her along with him.

Like all avoidants attached to ambivalents, she has to work at keeping a cool eye and receptive ear for the wheat and the chaff she's getting from her partner, and to trust her own solid and reliable instincts. If your inner voice tells you your partner is behaving like a misinformed hothead, you're probably right. Don't act on rash advice you don't quite trust.

Attempt to Eliminate the Critical Tone

This is a challenge for both the avoidant *and* the ambivalent partner.

Larry and Rachel described several mini-battles that underscore the difficulty they have adjusting to a change in the emotional status quo. When habitual interactions began to shift, it stirred anxiety in both partners.

Rachel had been thinking for some time about getting back to work. With the kids growing up, she knew she had to do something to shake those blue and listless moods. And Larry had been indicating he was all for it for some time.

He's a fellow who's very wrapped up in his job and community activities, getting much applause from the world for all that. Indeed, an avoidant will often seek outside applause, because he can garner feelings of appreciation and connectedness without expressions of intimacy. And he did think his wife should have something more going on, if for no other reason than that she'd be in a better mood and thus make life more pleasant for him. Periodically, he had come up with suggestions for her—How about selling real estate? How about being a museum docent? She didn't like any of his suggestions. And, understandably, she was a bit frightened about getting out in the job world again.

But Rachel started thinking how much she had enjoyed the graduate studies she had started and then dropped. She had enjoyed the long hours in the library and writing papers, thought she had a knack for a certain kind of scholarly endeavor, and was adept at using computers. Through her college placement office she obtained a job as a researcher for a history professor, working two to three afternoons a week.

She loved it—it was the perfect, low-key, easy re-entry situation for her. Since Larry had been encouraging her to start moving, and, finally, she'd made it happen, one would hope he'd say: "This is great that you've found something you like and enjoy and want to do. It sounds just right for you."

He did not. At the end of her first week on the job, Larry remarked: "So, what is it? You're getting minimum wage? Hardly seems worth it." His only comment was a little voice of criticism, a little put-down. Rachel was livid: "Fine, maybe I should just quit then."

She didn't, though. And Larry keeps using this dig to complain and be critical (and, of course, to express his fear of abandonment). When he has gripes about something not getting done in the house and Rachel says, "I worked longer hours today than I expected," he replies: "Then why don't you quit? You're not making any real money there anyway." Even in sessions with the counselor, this is a bone he can't let go of. "She's going to work, that's great," he says, "but she acts like she's reinvented the wheel here, like this is such a major deal."

It's easy to see that Larry is unnerved by his partner's altering the couple fit in becoming a better self-feeder. His major challenge at this juncture involves accepting the changing nature of their attachment by first eliminating the critical tone by which he attempts to avoid those changes.

And Rachel can help him along by mastering some lessons of her own. In her ambivalent's way, she's doing too much sniping and attacking: "Why do you keep saying that? You were the one telling me to find a job, to get out of the house more. Now I'm doing it and all I hear from you are criticisms." Certainly, it's easy to appreciate her annoyance at him. But her responses perpetuate the dance.

She might say instead: "You know, Larry, you're absolutely right. It's minimum wage, I'm not thrilled about that either and I'm hoping some day I'll make more. Maybe I will, maybe I won't. But that's not why I'm doing this. I'm finding that I love researching. It's right up my alley. And I'm good at it. So I'm not thrilled about the money but I am thrilled about the work. Isn't that great? And as I get more settled into the routine, I'll pick up some of these house things that I've had to let go by the board. Or we'll figure out how to do a little better advance planning together to see what needs to be done when."

In one fell swoop, she takes away his club. Nothing in those remarks will allow him to come right back at her with a hurtful observation. She's agreed with him—the salary is lousy. And she's further explained herself in a way he can't fault—I really love what I'm doing.

Several months after Rachel began working, and after we'd hashed over the preceding suggestions in our sessions, Larry gained some insight into his critical behavior vis-à-vis Rachel's job, and made (for him) a gargantuan effort to change his tune. When Rachel had a deadline to meet and needed to put in some uninterrupted at-home work hours over the course of a week, Larry suggested he come home early and take on the evening duties with their sons. He oversaw homework and TV watching and lights out.

Rachel was listening to all this with one ear. "The kids are so unused to seeing him around, they pay no attention to him," she explains in our session. "He tries to enforce rules, but he doesn't know how to do that. So the boys stayed up too late. And their backpacks weren't ready the next morning." Rachel came out picking at her partner, telling him how he *ought* to get the kids to behave. Larry responded, she tells us, by pointing out that she was "hardly a model of consistency in child-rearing policy herself" and by stomping off.

Rachel *did* want him to take care of things with their sons and *did* appreciate the time she was allowed, but she also couldn't resist finding fault. Thus, the fight. While Larry perhaps must oil his parenting skills, to engineer a better couple fit he needs to tell Rachel, nicely, to back off and not go on the attack. Next time, instead of picking up the fight, he might say: "Well, you're right, they were up late. But the main thing is, you've got to get your work done. How can we do this better? Maybe if the kids get their homework finished early, I can take them out for the evening so we won't distract you. What do you think?"

Now, he takes away her club, and, ideally, they shift to a more constructive line of behavior.

As you or your partner begins to get better at self-feeding and, perhaps, to act more independently, the emotional underpinnings of your couple fit start to change. Change can be uncomfortable, even anxiety-producing. And when you're anxious, it's easy to find fault and criticize. Eliminate the critical tone as you struggle to adjust to the new order of things.

Nudge Your Partner, When Necessary and to the Extent Possible, out of the Emotional and into the Intellectual Mode

You have an issue that must be addressed, a problem to solve, an action to take; you want your ambivalent partner to participate in the dilemma, and to offer support or be actively helpful. She, in typical emotional style, is ready to go into battle. But battling is counterproductive.

At one point, Jeanette's mother became ill with hard-to-pinpoint ailments and unsatisfactory diagnoses. Jeanette spent a lot of time over those several months stopping by her mother's apartment, on each occasion stirring up Kent's annoyance: "Don't keep going there so much," he'd say. "It's not necessary and you're exhausting yourself. Hire somebody to be with her, if you think it's so important. But it's not." Kent took the situation as another battle—he's going to protect his wife by keeping her from being exhausted. (And keep her always available to him, not abandoning him by going off to be with her mom.) And avoidant Jeanette, annoyed, would say only, "I've got to go over there tonight, but not for long."

In a perfect world, Kent, being supportive and helpful, might have said something like this: "Do what you think is best. Do what's in your heart. Maybe there's something I can get started around the house or something I can cover for you when you need to go to your mother's." On his own, he finds that difficult. But Jeanette can give him a little help, perhaps in this way: "You know, I'd really like to hear your thoughts on this. Do you think we should persuade Mom to go to a new internist? She's a little confused about what tests she's had already. Maybe we should try to get from her doctor a full accounting of what he's done. What do you think?" And so on. And then maybe her partner will come up with some genuinely useful, forward-moving thoughts.

When an ambivalent can shift out of the emotional field and stick to the intellectual one, he'll be able to make good judgments—identify the problem, come up with a suggested solution, and even see where he might pitch in. Help your ambivalent partner distance himself—put on another pair of shoes, assume a slightly different identity in a sense—and you will in all likelihood be delighted to watch him achieve the objectivity he needs, see the matter clearly, and participate constructively. In other words, ease him out of his own subjective shoes and into a more objective stance, and he can do an "as if"—act as if he's a reasonable, rational, secure individual.

And then stick to the issue, leaving off the negative. After your partner has stepped out of his shoes, say: "That's really helpful. You've seen the situation so clearly. I've got a much better fix on what to do."

Remember the Good Times

This is a key bit of advice for both the avoidant and the ambivalent, each of whom is likely to dismiss his or her partner's last six kind, thoughtful, loving, positive behaviors in light of the one new negative that's popped up.

Consider this example: A couple we counseled decided to restore some zing to their marriage by celebrating their fifth anniversary in a romantic spot. He, she said, should make all the plans, and he did—weekend reservations at a country inn, flowers waiting in the room, an excellent wine waiting at their dinner table. They ate, hiked, made love, and slept very well. Later, while driving home, they had the following conversation:

HE: Wasn't this a wonderful weekend? Didn't we have a great time?

SHE: Yes, it was wonderful. Except you didn't get me a present.

HE: Well . . . that never occurred to me. I mean, this whole weekend was the present.

SHE: I'm not saying it wasn't great. I was just expecting a present too.

He did six things right; she found the one that allowed her to toss them all out and send her partner and herself back to Go.

Try not to expect too much. Remember the good times. Hold on to them, internalize them, be grateful for them, speak of them.

CHAPTER 12

All Over the Emotional Map:

The Ambivalent/Ambivalent Couple

HE AND SHE

FROM moment one, this husband and wife—it's the second marriage for each—are on the attack. Each seems actively irritated over being here at all. Although they were both pleased to volunteer and expressed excitement about the project when they arrived, now as she looks over our list, she rolls her eyes in a little "Oh, for Pete's sake, what is this all about anyway?" display. They begin:

SHE: All right, let's start with this one—how do most of our arguments start? What do you think?

HE: Oh, you're running this? You're improvising?

SHE (rolling her eyes, wagging her head): Yes. I'm improvising. Unless you have a better idea.

HE: Fine.

SHE: Okay. . . . You let your son get away with murder. He's almost twenty years old, isn't it time he grew up a little?

HE: He knows what he's doing.

SHE: Didn't you give him money for a second freshman year? Yes or no?

HE: So? You do the same thing for Mary.

SHE: That really is a completely different situation.

HE: I don't see the difference. If you think Josh takes advantage of me, I'd say Mary takes advantage of you, all the time. When she's in town, she absorbs you completely. It's an excess of togetherness.

SHE: Look, when Josh wants to do something with us, you're thrilled. You get annoyed only because when my daughter takes my time, you're not the center of attention anymore. Most people would agree with me about that. My mother says so. Even your supposed best buddy Bob says that you want my undivided attention.

HE (*into the camera*): I married a woman with two crazy parents.

(*They've been looking at each other throughout this talk, as it continues its back-and-forth progress. Abruptly, she glares over at the camera, makes an "If you don't mind . . ." motion with her head and hands, and wrenches her chair around to sit looking directly at him. The camera and the therapist be damned!*

Having run the "how do our arguments start" issue to the ground, or to nowhere much at all, she takes up the list again.)

SHE: "Sex."

HE: Sex is fine, in my opinion.

SHE: Sex is fine. I do like to have sex. Of course also, it's the only thing that keeps you in a good mood.

HE: Oh please. I don't hear any complaints.

SHE: All right, another question. "Decisions about spending money."

HE: Do you think I'd like you to make more decisions about money?

SHE: It's not a question of making more decisions. You completely disempower me about spending money.

HE: Disempower? What are you talking about? I would rather buy more expensive things, I would rather you buy more expensive things. You've gone through three decorators already. How many chances do you get?

SHE: That's not what it's about.

HE: Of course it is, that's what people mean about spending money. For example, I'd like to buy fresh orange juice and you told me just the other day that you prefer to buy frozen because it's cheaper.

SHE: You can buy fresh orange juice anytime you want.

HE: I'm going to now, now that you said you're not going to get it any more. I didn't want to upset you by buying it before, but okay, now I'm going to.

SHE: Well, I won't drink it.

HE: Wait a minute. You told me yesterday to buy fresh-squeezed juice, and I did, and you drank it.

SHE: Yeah, once. But not as a habitual thing. It's not worth it.

HE: But you said you enjoyed it. We can certainly afford it.

SHE: What are you talking about? I enjoy frozen orange juice too. It's a matter of degree.

HE: Look, I presume you enjoy the fresh more than the

frozen, otherwise you wouldn't have told me to buy it.

SHE: I couldn't care less whether I ever have fresh orange juice or frozen orange juice again as long as I live.

(When their ten minutes are up, both appear simultaneously relieved and annoyed to see the therapist entering the room to lead them out for a break. Then comes the reconciliation.)

SHE: Well, what kind of contrived conversation do you want to have now?

HE: Let's talk about the money thing. We didn't finish that.

SHE: When it comes to your spending money, I feel absolutely powerless. Not I feel, I *am* powerless.

HE: I really don't understand what you're saying.

SHE: I'm saying that you will spend money any way you want, regardless of what I think.

HE: And don't you spend money regardless of how I feel about it?

SHE: Well, it would depend.

HE: No, it wouldn't. You know, for example, I prefer fresh orange juice, to take a mundane example. But you prefer frozen juice, so that's what you buy, that's the way you want to spend the money. Spending the way you want doesn't necessarily imply spending more, you could be spending less too. So you're deciding how that money is spent.

SHE *(with an exaggerated yawn)*: True. But that doesn't preclude you from knowing how the money is spent.

HE: No. Out of respect for you, I don't buy fresh orange juice.

SHE: All right, now we're talking about fresh orange juice and frozen orange juice.

HE: It's just an example. What would you talk about? Give me another example.

SHE: What I said before, how you spend on Josh.

HE: Okay. Forget about that for now. How about what you spend on clothes? Do I ever tell you to spend less or to spend more? Do I question you about it?

SHE: No.

(The therapist comes in to say time's up.)

Some real issues are afoot here—a big one, that she raises, concerns her perceived lack of power. But with all the din, neither can hear much of anything; each pays little real attention to what the other is saying. He just wants to prove her wrong; she just wants to prove him wrong.

About the sex, there are, it seems, no complaints. Which is often the case for ambivalent/ambivalent couples, as we'll talk about later in this chapter. But here she won't receive the fact that maybe he wants sex because he wants *her*. Sex, not her, puts him "in a good mood."

She gets in the last words about the sex; he gets in the last words about money, spinning off into a long argument about orange juice. She's actually reaching here for an emotional content, which concerns how she feels he deprives her of her share of responsibility for their financial life and how therefore he wields the clout in the family. But once they get going with the great orange juice debate, the energy pours into out-arguing each other and keeping the battle heated.

Both demonstrate the ambivalent's need to go on the attack, hit below the belt, and always, always keep it personal. They're willing to drag in "crazy parents" and a possibly disloyal best friend to zing it to each other.

SUSAN AND JACK

"I took one look at him, and that was it," says Susan. She and Jack are both actors, the struggling variety, who patch together a good-enough living by waiting tables. Jack also plays occasional gigs for a few hundred dollars with a rock band he started in college, and Susan sells handmade silver and semi-precious stone rings at street fairs. They are both exceptionally gorgeous, especially Jack, who in addition to all the other plates he has in the air lands an occasional catalog modeling job.

While waiting for their "big break" on TV or in theater, they seem genuinely to enjoy their somewhat ragtag, "who knows what comes next?" existence. They've been living together for three years.

Susan was a rebel, even a bit of a daredevil, in her high school days in placid suburban New Jersey. She had a tough time with her parents, especially her disapproving father; hung out with a motorcycle crowd; and was thrilled to be accepted to a mid-level, prestigious, very liberal northeastern college. As she describes it, she metamorphosed instantly "from black leather biker chick to artsy actress and crafts-woman." Loving everything to do with the theater, she moved to New York after graduation, and met Jack her first week there at a walk-in audition for "some mean streets urban movie with a nonspeaking cast of a few thousand." He was attracted to her, she was smitten with him. Susan made up her mind to get Jack.

It's a not unusual getting-together story for two ambivalents, who can become quickly, intensely infatuated. They conjure up a love partner ideal, maybe go along with a lot of nonsense from each other at the start—the nonsense being exciting, lovable even! Or, they may jointly be on their best behavior (during the early stages of being "in love," the majority of individuals, of whatever attachment styles, act well). Or, typically, one will be, unconsciously, laying very low during the courtship days, instinctively toning things down, not revealing what he or she really thinks or wants, busily positioning the other for "the catch."

Susan was the catcher. While she bowled Jack over with her beauty, sense of fun, and sexiness, it seemed to him also she deemed him just perfect. A few years down the road, however, things were not so pleasant anymore.

"I'm living with Jekyll and Hyde," Susan said in our first session. "Jack blows a gasket one minute; an hour later, he's all cuddly and cozy. His rages seem completely off the wall and out of nowhere."

"Off the wall and out of nowhere" is a pretty good description of what apparently goes on between Jack and Susan. Two things had happened to bring the ambivalent/ambivalent pattern to the surface in this relationship. First, Susan, past her sweetheart phase, was showing her neediness and dependency. This is not so terrible—in some ways, Jack's ready to handle it. He is protective of her vis-à-vis her father; he's always there when her family is around (and they often are), serving as a buffer zone; and he talks her through the aftermath of meetings with her parents, which generally get her blood boiling.

"She wants to get it out of her system, but then she picks apart something I said and tells me I insulted her family," Jack says. He's also angry because, as he describes it, "we both agree she's the bigger scatterbrain, and I'm the one who has to keep some semblance of order in our lives. So, for example, I mostly shop for the food, but then it's not what she wants." He feels unappreciated, put down by her.

Adding a further charge to the prevailing atmosphere is the second change this couple has experienced. Jack, since his college days, had enjoyed marijuana, virtually every evening. Although he didn't think of it in these terms, he'd been self-medicating to keep calm. Six months before these two came to see us, he had decided to stop this habit. Jack's current mood swings are less predictable than ever, and not necessarily triggered, as Susan points out, by something going on in the moment.

PHIL AND SALLY

Sally runs a small, flourishing antiques business, a shop she opened once the couple's two sons were old enough not to need full-time attention. Phil is a salesman for a medical supplies company, so he does a bit of traveling.

Right now, the issue on the table concerns summer plans for their oldest boy, thirteen-year-old Tim.

PHIL: I want Timmy to go to sleep-away camp. He wasn't ready for it before, but now he is. Most of his friends are going away. He says he wants to go. You and I *(looking daggers at Sally)* agreed on this. Now all of a sudden *(looking daggers at the counselor)* she's changing her mind. She tells Timmy he doesn't have to go if he doesn't want to, it's up to him, he can wait until next year.

SALLY: That's not what I said. I said I don't know about that particular camp that you've got all picked out.

PHIL: But you agreed about this camp. We said we want him to get away so he's not just hanging around over the summer, and we want him in a sports camp.

SALLY: Well, this place sounds too competitive.

After listening to some further back-and-forth, we ask what Tim's thoughts on the subject are. On that, they agree: "He doesn't know what he wants."

Clearly, we can say, these parents need to make an important decision for their child, encouraging his input to an appropriate degree. But the possibility of taking a joint parental action seems beyond Sally and Phil. Once in agreement, these two ambivalents tend to begin undermining and undoing, leaving them back at square one.

We'd been down similar roads before, because Sally and Phil have been coming for counseling—off and on—for twelve years, almost as long as they've been married. Today we talk summer camp. Other times, it's been friends, karate lessons, where to vacation, when to buy a bigger house. Frequently, it's been about Phil's traveling.

Although Sally doesn't relish having her husband around all that much and he's not so happy to be there (this is not some honeybunch household), much unpleasantness surfaces when he leaves. For example, Phil announced recently that he had an out-of-state sales presentation to make. He would be flying out Thursday evening and doing the job Friday. He thought he would then stay over to get in a little golf and swimming on Saturday, and catch an early Sunday plane back.

We'd think Sally might enjoy a little respite herself, and look forward to the peace and quiet. To the contrary, she began chipping away—why leave on Thursday if you don't have to be there until Friday? and so on. The upshot: Although between the lines he had been announcing to her, "I'm looking forward to getting away from you and staying away even longer to enjoy myself," Phil scuttled his plans, agreeing to leave later, on Friday, and come back earlier, on Saturday.

At the heart of that contradictory behavior is a powerful

fear of abandonment, on each partner's part. And yet, despite those abandonment issues, Sally and Phil routinely threaten divorce, especially Sally, who every so often says, "Look what you're doing to the kids, we can't go on this way." He's more afraid of divorce, and when the threats come, he tends impulsively to roar off to their summer cabin and spend a day or two ferociously throwing himself into house repairs. Sally never knows when Phil will disappear or turn up again—the ambivalent's escapes, unlike the avoidant's, are rarely predictable.

Although each swears the only way to resolve their difficulties is through divorce or separation, Sally and Phil are unlikely to do either. And although they participate animatedly in couples therapy, it seems they come not really to resolve the thorny issue of the moment, but to air the dissatisfaction and prolong the upheaval. Only lately have they been able to begin to recognize that.

YOLANDA AND ALEX

When Yolanda married Alex six years ago, she thought she "had died and gone to heaven." It is the first marriage for thirty-five-year-old Yolanda and the second for Alex, who's forty-nine. A heavenly aspect still wafts at times around this relationship—always in evidence after one of their periodic blowups, which is then followed by an ensuing period of mutual bliss. Once the storm is over, they both apologize, have some marvelous sex, and then embark on a period of days or weeks of absolute euphoria. Each can't believe his or her good fortune in being with this exceptional partner. They have dates, spending romantic evenings at supper clubs listening to the piano player sing love songs.

Alex, a successful lawyer with his own practice, makes a

pile of money. Although a large chunk of it goes in alimony to his former wife, there's an even heftier chunk left over. Yolanda, an ethereal-looking woman with a mass of strawberry-blond curls, teaches little tots in a Montessori school. While her husband presents the solid, confident, out-there aggressiveness we might expect in a self-made, self-employed rich guy, Yolanda is an unusual mix—a little dithery in the way she talks but with a mind as sharp as a tack; a glamorous dresser who loves working with little kids and has a strong domestic, even earthy streak.

They're having big fights about money, they explain, mainly about his alimony payments. And more big fights about setting up their apartment. They wish for fewer of the fights and more of the euphoria.

The apartment, it seems, should hardly be a problem. It's a big, roomy place with three bedrooms, one of which they decided should be her in-house office.

"I bought a desk, a floor lamp, a couch, and a few other pieces of furniture," says Yolanda, "and got the room set up the way I wanted it. And he can't stay out of it!" Alex has taken to spreading himself out in there, sometimes literally—she found him taking a Sunday afternoon nap in "her" office last week. She was furious.

"I have no problem with her taking over this room, and if she wants to think of it as an office, fine," says Alex testily. "It's this absurd possessiveness of hers, berating me for taking a nap when she wasn't even using the room."

From our He and She conversation and our three couples, we can paint a picture of this couple combination, one with lots of vivid reds and oranges, jarring blacks, and quite a few zigzagging, slashing lines! Think of Rhett Butler and Scarlett O'Hara in Margaret Mitchell's *Gone With the Wind*, perhaps our classic ambivalent/ambivalent pair. From start to finish, you'll recall, these two can't decide whether to fight or make love or do both simultaneously. Neither has a solid grasp of appropriate boundaries—she seduces her sister's fiancé and chases after her friend's husband; he switches political allegiance as business dictates. Coming together, then bounding apart, like twisting magnets, even the tragic loss of their daughter finds them unable to comfort each other.

The relationship of two ambivalents is a lively affair. In counseling, this couple will often immediately attempt to make the environment their own. Like the visiting mother-in-law who rearranges the furniture without asking, ambivalent clients tend to take over the space they will inhabit, even for an hour. Susan chooses a chair, moves it a foot closer to us, then shoves it back. Jack rushes in late with his take-out bag, drags over a small table, spreads out his coffee and blueberry muffin, and announces, "I'm going to need this!"

At home, two ambivalents similarly intrude on each other's territory—like Alex sprawling out in his wife's designated room—without permission or any real awareness of intrusiveness. Boundaries, to put it mildly, are fluid. Seemingly unable to accept things as they are, these two at once challenge the status quo.

It's an exhilarating relationship, especially in the beginning, which is filled with passion, sex, and adventure. Like Susan, the ambivalent meeting a potential partner may at once become engrossed in "making the catch," in the thrill of the chase. And for all the subsequent battling that usually characterizes the pattern, a sense of liveliness frequently prevails, because nothing is fixed and something is always happening. Although these couples can glare, insult, threaten, and withhold, they will also, in a flash, laugh, flirt, and play.

While the downs are very down, the ups can be tremendous, like the euphoria Yolanda and Alex want to sustain.

The whirlpooling emotions help this pair feel attached. Without all the mercurial activity, they experience feelings of anxiety and loss—or perhaps, more obviously, of boredom and monotony.

Ambivalents are tough to work with in therapy—exhausting, in fact. But they're also fun. Fights are out in the open; sassy talk is in the air. Encouraging revelations is easy; they do engage with each other and with the therapist. But living in the ambivalent/ambivalent relationship can be like swimming against the tide; nobody gets anywhere. And nobody can fall asleep in that household!

Arguments take the form of tests that must result in failure. Each seems to be saying: Tell me what you want me to do so I won't do it. Because ambivalent behavior is rooted in opposing someone, two ambivalents will try to defeat one another (and the therapist as well; they work at taking away the counselor's power to be of help). There will be criticism without resolution or reconciliation. There is never a position taken and stuck with, or a very clear "yes" or "no." Neither gets what he or she wants, or is happy with the compromise.

That supercharged atmosphere isn't really fun to live in, over time. Anxiety, rather than genuine enthusiasm for the events of the day, drives all the excitement, and the fallout is often difficult and painful for children or other close relations.

To give up the drive to keep the fight going, though, and then to work at recreating the fit, is difficult and unfamiliar to these people. As therapists, our goal focuses on moving the ambivalent/ambivalent couple toward a little greater containment, with an emphasis on the "little greater." Once they can tone down the worst of the bad behavior—the criticism, the attacks, and the minimizing—a safer, more genuinely comfortable environment for themselves and their families begins to emerge.

TOWARD A MORE COMFORTABLE COUPLE FIT

Cease the Ultimate Threats

About once a month, Sally says, "I'm leaving, I'm getting a divorce." Like many ambivalents, she enjoys that flirtation with noncommitment—today I'm announcing that I'm leaving Phil, although I love him. Ultimatums serve the purpose of keeping the chaotic atmosphere alive and well.

So here's our first and simplest recommendation for ambivalent pairs who routinely threaten divorce: Stop doing that.

Decide you will issue no more *ultimate* comments and threats.

If you are on the receiving end of such an ultimatum or threat, call your partner's bluff. Say: "Are you really serious about this idea of divorce? If you are, then why not call a divorce lawyer, find out what your rights are? Get some solid information."

When you call his bluff, you take away your partner's club; you're saying you are not scared and you will not be threatened.

Don't Use the Kids

"You were the one who signed up Paul for Sunday school," says Phil to his partner during one of our sessions. "He doesn't want to go; he should have a say in this. I was the one who calmed everything down, because you couldn't handle it."

"But hold on a minute," says Sally. "Two weeks later, you're telling him, 'Get ready for Sunday school—come on, let's get moving.' "

Sally's working up some steam on this issue of who's the kinder, gentler parent: "The kids are scared of you. Both of them told me they don't want to ride with you because you drive like a crazy man. I had to take them to practice last weekend because they don't want to drive with you."

For this couple, as for many married ambivalent pairs, the children are vehicles for arguing. Neither Mom nor Dad is really overly interested in whether it's right for everybody— their sons and themselves as a family—for Timmy to attend camp, or how to get the kids to sports practice in a timely fashion, or why Paul should or should not have piano lessons or go to Sunday school. As parents, they have difficulty focusing on a resolution to their children's problems or on thrashing out appropriate decisions concerning actions to take. Primarily intent on keeping the fight going, husband and wife are each capable of using a child's need or distress to prove what's wrong with the other.

And yet each couple would be shocked to hear that they were "using" their children in this way. Ask any ambivalent parent, and he or she will say, "Of course, I only want what's best for my kid!" But truly, in the thick of their spousal battle for control and "being right," what's best for the child comes low on the list. They hardly know how to begin to discuss it.

So we try to bring them around to that discovery in a somewhat oblique way. We might say: "It seems important to you that you have a lot of justification for your position and your actions concerning the children." Or, with what we hope is a lighthearted tone: "Poor Paul. His mom and dad are spending a lot of time arguing instead of deciding whether he's a good candidate for piano lessons." If it works, our remarks will bring them up short a bit, give them pause, and nudge them toward a more constructive track.

Do you need to bring yourself up short a bit? If lots of arguments between you and your mate have a he-says/she-says context centering on your offspring, resolve to stop using your children to keep the fight going. When a decision concerning your child must be made, sit together, talk it out partner to partner, and then present a united front to your offspring.

Establish a Greater Degree of Sexual Containment

Two of our three couples have somewhat offbeat sexual practices, which is not terribly unusual for the ambivalent/ambivalent pair. Jack, for example, wants sex with Susan at least once a day. In the first year or two, she was all for it. Now, although sex is a powerful part of her personality and motivations, she's not always so willing.

"If I didn't love Susan as much as I do," says Jack, "there's a word I'd use for her." He describes some teasing, provocative behaviors on her part, with no follow-through. And now Susan rushes to let us—her partner and her counselor—know that she's just as hot as he is, even if she doesn't always want what he wants when he wants it. She masturbates "almost every day," she says. And there's something else too: She enjoys an evening out with a girlfriend from time to time at a topless bar, where they flirt with men. "Nothing happens, of course," she says. Jack didn't know about the masturbating. He did know about the girls' nights out, because Susan tells him afterward and then they have some great sex.

It seems clear that Susan uses her sexual availability to

wield some control over her partner: Will she or won't she tonight, he wonders? And do those anonymous flirtations have to stir her up before I get her?

Yolanda and Alex briefly toyed with the idea of alternative sexual practices, and once went as far as to invite another couple for a *ménage à quatre* (everybody ended up having a lot to drink and feeling less interested in the possible escapade). They mention that evening during one of our sessions, smiling at each other—the idea apparently still sounds tempting.

We say flat-out: Stop with the topless bars and the four-in-a-bed notions. Such behaviors will push the envelope too far and ultimately undermine the relationship.

Uncontained sexual liaisons are acting out through sex: What are the limits? What will I get away with? What will my partner accept? But two ambivalents don't really need outside titillation to resolve any sexual diffidences between them (as, for example, two avoidants might rent a porn video to get things going). What they do need is to turn the heat down a little and begin to accept the inevitably tamer flavor of an ongoing love life.

Ambivalent partners who like sex a lot have trouble with that tamer flavor. They want the high back, and if it takes outrageous behavior to get higher, so be it. That, of course, is what spurs on some of the fights, to be followed by some of the euphoric reunions. But, as we've noted, the rush to sexual reconnection deflects attention from an issue that probably needs that attention. As any relationship continues and matures into a deeper, more complex kind of intimacy, sex should become one of a variety of satisfactions, not a means of acting out.

Establish Hands-Off Boundaries

We use "hands-off" in the particular meaning of possessions and in the broader sense of territory and responsibilities. As an ambivalent, you very possibly lack an intuitive sense of personal privacy and of space. Thus, you may find it all too easy to tell your partner what to wear, when to sleep, and why he should get off the phone with his sister. Boundaries are hard for you to recognize, much less respect.

Susan and Jack quickly pinpointed a handful of small, irritating intrusions each made into the other's "territory." Susan wore his favorite sweatshirt all the time, without asking. Jack used her hairbrush. Resolving to stop these habits was the beginning of the major challenges for them of establishing stronger emotional boundaries and setting limits.

Draw up and talk over your own lists of irritating intrusions, keeping the emphasis on *intrusions*. You do not want to indulge in a rundown of each other's annoying practices—he drinks milk right from the container, she starts humming when she gets annoyed. If you go down that road, you're likely to start ringing up a rash of accusations—"You really want to be back in your bachelor pad where you lived like a pig," "You have no intention of listening to what I'm saying so you hum me out." Address such annoyances at some point when you've become much more adept at respecting the simple boundaries that should separate you—this is my hairbrush, my sweatshirt, my phone call with my sister, so keep your distance.

Look at each other and say, "I want you to stop XYZ." Do a little negotiating over responsibilities—okay, you'll do the marketing (your space), I'll do the cooking (my space). Stay in your respective spaces; consider those neutral corners. Don't get so mixed up in each other.

Make a Deal

Making a deal takes establishing boundaries a bit further. It may not be especially troublesome for Susan and Jack to stick to their agreement that it's hands off the sweatshirt and the hairbrush, but they have a harder time keeping to understandings over more emotionally inflammatory issues, such as what role he should or should not play in her family involvements.

Those boundaries, even if each knows what they are or should be, get blurry very quickly. Then one or the other might need to push once more for further containment; to foster, in other words, the partner's ability to self-regulate. Jack might say: "Look, we know that after some of the usual nonsense has gone on between you and your family, you come at me like gangbusters. You can't do that. If you have a hard time containing yourself, maybe that's the time you should go out for a jog. Or go to the gym." Susan might say: "I know I have a hard time with my father, but that's really my problem. And I think part of what goes on is that you get a little jealous or threatened about that situation, and you butt in too much, maybe when I don't want you to. You can't do that. So I'm going to tell you when you need to back off."

An ambivalent isn't terribly good at limiting himself or herself. Self-regulating is tough. But these two can help each other; they can say, "I'll put a limit on you, you put a limit on me."

Decide what deal you need to make. Enforce a bit more containment on the picture. Even if deeper issues and problems need attention, making a deal is fine for the time being.

What's Done, Just Leave Alone

Yolanda hung a newly purchased, framed museum print in the front hallway, with Alex's approval. A week later, she returned from a two-day teacher's conference and found that Alex had moved the print into the kitchen. She got mad. Then he got mad at her for getting mad.

Here is the ambivalent pair's constant pas de deux of doing and then undoing. Nothing is ever left alone; nothing is ever finally completed. In fact, many ambivalent/ambivalent couples tend to *accomplish* less than other pairs. At no point are they able to announce, "Okay, that's done, now we move on to something else." Ambivalents may live in empty houses, because they never agree on furniture. Conversely, they sometimes inhabit houses stuffed to the gills, unable to decide what to put up or take down.

Behind all the doing and undoing is the powerful drive never to achieve a feeling of inner satisfaction and always to maintain that element of chaos. There is forever something to be resolved, and if he resolves it, she unresolves it. It's a kind of bee's nest going on here—somebody's always buzzing around and neither just enjoys the honey. This, of course, is where the ambivalent/ambivalent passion lies, whence comes the feeling of life. But all that buzzing can take a heavy toll over time.

If you've started to think about drawing some boundary lines; if you've negotiated a few distinctive territories you each will separately inhabit; and especially if you've made a decision or reached a conclusion, then try now to recognize what should be left alone. If your partner has done it, consider it done.

Ask Yourself, "Is Something *Really* Wrong, Terrible, and Impossible Here?"

With two ambivalents, little explosions pop off like fire-crackers, right and left, hither and yon. They like it that way, but lots of constantly popping little explosions add up to an unhappily overheated, angry atmosphere.

Here's a fight that went on for some time between Phil and Sally. Sally flossed her teeth in bed at night, a habit her partner abhorred, and he told her. She, keeping the buzzing going, continued her bedtime flossing. Sometimes in the morning he found a bit of used floss in the sheets.

Phil, although he was constantly getting up a real head of steam on this, decided he'd play nice one evening.

PHIL: Don't you think you could do that in the bathroom?

SALLY: Well, you cut your toenails on the edge of the bed.

PHIL: Where the hell do you think I *should* cut my toenails?

SALLY: Look, if my dental floss is disgusting to you, your toenail cutting is equally disgusting to me!

PHIL: When I clip my toenails, afterward I brush all the clippings into the trash basket. You leave your floss in the bed!

One round to Phil.

It's easy to see, at this reflective remove, the childishness to their argument, which devolves into who performs his and her disgusting habit more considerately. It's easy to see the intensity of the rage that rises up over the littlest thing. And maybe we can see, too, that all this angry positioning helps each one feel a bit more puffed up, a bit more powerful and stronger than he or she in fact is.

But the over-the-top feelings *are* real. Ambivalents feel things, hard; they have intensified reactions. As counselors, one of our hardest tasks is to get the ambivalent pair to come to see when they're overreacting, to take a step back and recognize a lot of overexcitement about nothing much at all. So we'll say something like this: "I see it's upsetting you to have this situation going on. What you feel is real. But just because you feel it doesn't mean that the issue itself is such a four-star crisis. Do you think there are more intense feelings surfacing here than the situation warrants?" And, taking a step back, they often can answer yes.

Consider your own littlest-things arguments. Ask yourself, "Is something *really* terribly wrong here?" If you can't answer "yes," simmer down. The relationship of two ambivalents can involve much acting out without listening, and little acceptance of small differences. There are lots of dramas over not much of anything.

Express Positive Feelings—Only Positive Feelings

This is an immensely difficult assignment for a pair of ambivalents. In session, at some point along the way—usually after a number of meetings during which this man and woman have vented a litany of complaints against each other—we'll pose this question: "What is it you don't resent about your partner? We've heard now all the things you *do* resent—what don't you?"

They have to stop and think about that one. And then they'd just as soon not talk about it, since they find more satisfaction in fixating on the gripes. Yolanda will run on for ten minutes about how she spent the afternoon cooking yellow split pea soup with smoked ham hocks, Alex's favorite, and then he didn't make the effort to put the napkins and bowls out on the table. The fact that he puts a high six-figure income on the table doesn't signify in some way, or need not be acknowledged.

When Sally and Phil jointly decided their son would go to camp and the camp he would go to, we said: "This is great. You've resolved the issue. Now for the next week, express to each other positive feelings around that issue. Don't question it. Don't undo it. And if you have negative feelings about this done issue, do not voice them."

Remember the accomplishment, we're saying; tamp down your urge to find something again to resent or to rehash. Accentuate the positive, and only the positive. This is a different bit of advice than that we'd offer the avoidant, who needs encouragement in acknowledging and expressing *all* his feelings, the positive and negative. Ambivalents are right at home with the negative stuff. Flipping to the other side of the coin is harder.

In your own ambivalent relationship, try this: For one day, express only positive feelings toward your partner. It might actually feel rather pleasant. You might even be tempted to try it for a week.

Or, if that's too difficult, put a more positive spin on a negative observation here and there. Instead of, "These directions can't be right. You must have gotten the wrong information," say, "Are you sure this is the right way? I could have sworn we go the other way, but maybe I'm getting turned around." You see the goal here—to diffuse some of the conflict-laden, oppositional tone of your normal daily intercourse. A positive spin was, perhaps, what Phil was attempting in his question to Sally with the flossing: "Don't you think you could do that in the bathroom?" This was certainly better than, "The way you floss your teeth is revolting," but it nevertheless carried a hostile and accusatory ring that undermined his efforts. We'd suggest for him a more lighthearted approach, relying on an "I-message," something like: "I think it's great that you're determined to take good care of your teeth. I would like it a lot, however, if you conducted the flossing business in the bathroom."

To find the positive, or more of it, give some thought to what unites you. There is always something—probably many somethings, or you wouldn't be together. It is as simple as asking, "What do we have in common?" You value family ties, or you enjoy making a nice home, or you want your kids to get a first-class education. Say something positive around what unites you.

Resolve to Curb the *Who's Afraid of Virginia Woolf* Scenes

Once an argument starts, two ambivalents will pull out all the stops. They can be cruel.

In session, it's often an effective tactic to ask two ambivalents to reflect on life in the family home when they were kids. Recall typical little scenes between you and each of your parents, we'll suggest. What was the fit back then? Do you see any patterns, any similarities between what went on with you and your parents and what goes on with you and your partner today? Such reflections often lead our ambivalents to draw some eye-opening connections.

Susan described her mother as "either sweet or bitchy," often both in virtually the same breath. For Susan's seventeenth birthday, her mom bought her a navy blue cashmere pullover that Susan had lusted after in a department store catalog. Susan, thrilled with the sweater, wore it on a date with her boyfriend that evening. Mom said Susan looked gorgeous, then added: "You don't have much there to fill it out; you really ought to shop for a padded bra." The mean streak surfaces, perhaps unintentionally. Mom, not having notions of affection and closeness straight in her own head, wished to be generous and loving, then was compelled to smash that accomplishment with a castaway criticism. It's the old ambivalent's need to give and to take away, to use the sword instead of the kiss.

Sally and Phil took to this idea of the sword and the kiss. They got it, and were able—with a surprising degree of self-awareness and insight—to spot and describe their own fluctuations along these lines. Phil said: "I think with Sally, most times I get the kiss and *then* I get the sword. And the sword has a more powerful effect. It hurts! I suppose I do exactly the same thing to her."

Work at losing the sword. Decide there will be no more below-the-belt attacks, no more throwing old hurts into each other's faces. Try to remove the words "You always . . ." and "You never . . ." from arguments. Scrapping will always be part of your life; you need the perpetual tug-of-war, because without all the noise you feel a little anxious or a little bored. As we've noted, arguments occur not so much to resolve a problem, but rather as your means of staying close. And of course, after the fights, the reconnections are so often delicious. But you can, and must, eliminate the cruelty.

We advise our ambivalent couples to make a few ground rules. When life is calm, not when you're in the thick of an unpleasant bit of business, talk together about setting more limits: These are two things we're not going to say the next time we get in a fight. One of them might be dragging up a third-party "confirmation" of some failing or shortcoming of the other guy, as the wife in our He and She opening dialogue did by saying, even your best friend thinks you're a worm. It's a typical ambivalent's tactic, to "prove" herself right by lining up on her side this outside ammunition. And it's cruel.

Call a Time-Out

Here's another way to bring down the heat once an argument gives signs of going beyond the pale.

This classic technique that parents apply to unruly children worked well for Susan and Jack, somewhat to their surprise. When one of their battles was clearly escalating, one or the other was able to say, "Time! No more for now," and walk away. Avoidants, as we know, have a tough time staying with a discussion or argument that's getting uncomfortable; they have to make themselves stay in the fray. The fray is no problem for two ambivalents, however, and sometimes they do themselves well to move out of it, at least temporarily.

Leave the house if you possibly can—together. A change of venue helps things simmer down. Go out to a movie or a restaurant. Be together in a neutral place that will impose some restrictions and, ideally, enable you to talk without shouting.

Gird Yourself Emotionally for Times of Separation

Separations hit ambivalents hard. They react with anger.

Every Monday Alex visits one or two out-of-town clients, usually returning home the following day. And every Sunday, Yolanda and Alex get into a fight. She describes one such Sunday evening: "We were going to go to the movies and then get something to eat. I was feeling really close to Alex. We had the evening planned. We're sitting on the couch all snuggled up together, looking through the newspaper listings. I picked something I wanted to see, and all of a sudden Alex announced he doesn't want to go to the movies after all. I was furious. He's always changing plans, ruining a good time."

The argument escalated, then they ended up in bed having sex. Afterward, relaxing, Yolanda pointed out to Alex that he never apologized about "ruining" their evening. He said he didn't think he had to. As Alex left the next morning, these two were still arguing over whether or not he owed her an apology. They separated mad.

We can see that for Yolanda and Alex and for Phil and Sally (she who complains when he's around, then pesters him to come back earlier when he's gone), there's a fight when one of them goes away. Separation is a time to act out unreasonably, because separation means abandonment.

If you hear some familiar chords here, if the generally charged atmosphere in your relationship tends to spike up to dangerous levels when one of you has to be gone for a while, be forewarned. Make some advance plans of your own for that time. Get a change of scene—go out somewhere or spend time with friends the night before—so your abandonment issues don't come crashing down just as one of you is packing the suitcase.

Appreciate Each Other's Strengths

Name those strengths out loud; use them; rely on them. It's part of finding out what you *don't* resent about your partner, and it's part of drawing boundaries, not moving into each other's territory, stopping the doing-and-undoing pas de deux.

Consider Alex and Yolanda. One would deem these two a good match in the job area of life. He's doing the work he wants to do and making big bucks; she's doing the work she wants to do and making small bucks. But although Alex is such a highly successful man, he was oblivious to lots of bookkeeping and other matters that needed doing to keep things running smoothly. Fortunately, Yolanda had a bookkeeping soul and took over many of these chores, which included some invaluable assistance in organizing his business affairs. With lengthy vacations from her teaching, she had the time to devote to this and enjoyed herself acting as his unofficial office manager at home.

He does what she can't do and she does what he can't do. Instead of being satisfied with their arrangement and more-than-comfortable lifestyle, they fight. She harps on the alimony issue—to no purpose, since by law these payments must be made. He harps on her "fussing" with details.

How much pleasanter life would be if they could reach a point where they acknowledge and are grateful for each other's strengths. If Yolanda could say: "I really appreciate that you work as hard as you do, and provide us and everybody you're responsible for with such a comfortable living. It means I can do what I love without worrying about my income." If Alex could say: "I really appreciate that you're good at details. I know I have no eye for some of this, and your taking over the bookkeeping means I don't have to worry about things."

In your ambivalent/ambivalent relationship, keep chopping away at your tendencies to underappreciate each other. View yourselves as being on the same team, as indeed you are and must be if the relationship is to succeed. Focus on defined common goals. Lower the oppositional tone of daily life. Stop saying "Yes, but. . . ." Stick to "Yes."

Jack, speaking for himself and his lover, who nods in agreement, said this: "We're both difficult people. No one else has ever been able to put up with either of us for very long. We might as well figure out how to put up with each other."

Appreciating each other's strengths is a good start—and, somewhat paradoxically, invariably enhances the self-appreciation of each partner. We said at the start that an ambivalent has trouble achieving feelings of inner satisfaction: the sense of a job well done, a problem resolved, a decision made, or simply an enjoyable activity. In your ambivalent/ambivalent love relationship, you'll tend to search for that personal sense of satisfaction from each other, looking to your partner for a nod of approval or a frown of disapproval—and seldom find either for very long.

For more harmony and a less fractious daily life, work at achieving a greater degree of self-determination, a few more degrees of separation from your partner. Release some of the mutual dependency of your couple fit. Strive to experience a greater sense of internal satisfaction. Learn to feed yourself.

Afterword:
What Love Has to Do with It

HERE, now, one final couple fit for you to ponder:

Everyone envied Alice and Harry's marriage.

He was a much respected professor of classics at a prominent liberal arts college. She taught dance and beginning theater classes at a nearby state university. They threw wonderful parties—a Halloween costume bash each year, an elegant New Year's Eve get-together with good champagne and Harry's oyster stew, an end-of-the-academic-year "spring fiesta" cookout in June. Alice dressed her petite, lithe, dancer's body in clingy, jewel-toned silk shirts and slacks or short-shorts and halter tops—at the age of forty-two, she could still appear fifteen years younger. Harry, five years older than his wife, looked the stereotypical tweedy academic, tall and rangy and complete with pipe and leather elbow patches. From all appearances, their friends and colleagues thought they had a real love thing going on and that they were made for each other.

In many ways, such was the case.

Harry came from a rigid, punitive background, with a minister father who ran the show and a put-upon, suppressed, uptight mother. From his earliest years, he'd learned to deny all recognition or display of feelings; life ran more comfortably for him that way and he felt safer. Alice's father was a low-rung career officer in the diplomatic service, who moved his wife and only child to a new post every couple of years. A generally well-functioning alcoholic, he also sometimes turned abusive and once punched preteenaged Alice in the face. Her mother was a depressive, an unreliable source of comfort or direction for her daughter, and Alice lit out from home as soon as she could.

An extremely pretty young woman, she led a madcap existence in New York City, studying dance by day and partying at night with a succession of boyfriends and lovers, whom she'd captivate then dump. In her early twenties, she decided it would be wise to leave New York for a while, and on impulse she applied for and won a teaching assistant's job in the dramatic arts department of a suburban community college. There she crossed paths with her husband-to-be, Harry, who had recently earned his Ph.D. and was starting out on the academic career he already knew would be his life's calling and his great pleasure.

Eighteen years of marriage and two daughters later, Harry and Alice were doing okay . . . mostly. In many ways, her avoidant husband was a godsend for ambivalent Alice, the steadying force in her life. He was as straight an arrow as they come, an always reliable man. Sometimes he'd make a little fun of her, lightly ridiculing her in front of the children: "There goes Mom again, getting all wrought up about nothing much," he'd say. Sometimes she'd poke at him to talk more, express his feelings more, or tell her he loved her more: "Can you stop being so damn calm and inscrutable all the time?" she'd say. But it was not by accident that these two got together. They complemented each other, they were a good pair in public, and overall, it was a decent couple fit.

There were signs, however, that the fit might not hold. In the last several years Alice was starting to flip her cards. She had affairs, two one-afternoon stands in a motel a few miles from her campus. Then, bringing it all really close to home, she began a romance with a colleague of her husband's, even occasionally inviting the man and his wife to one of her dinner parties—pushing the envelope, shoving it in her husband's face, acting out. She knew that if she "got caught," Harry would be devastated, and she would despair, since she loved him and their life together. She knew all along, too, that she would never tell him and he would never ask or guess. And she wondered why on earth she needed to do what she was doing.

The truth was, little passion prevailed in the marriage. Lately, Alice often launched into vitriolic attacks on Harry, desperate to get a reaction. Once, going after whatever she could get hold of, she had said to him, "Are you homosexual or something?" Another time: "You know, Harry, I doubt you'd notice if I walked into the room stark naked. But we wouldn't want you to get too excited, bad for your cool image. Maybe I should get a boyfriend." And then, appalled at herself, she was quick to make up. And the pressure would build again, creating a cycle.

Alice was one angry woman. The appeal of the affair with Harry's colleague lay not so much in the exciting or titillating element of risk. Rather, the romance satisfied—briefly— her need to feel a sense of love, to express passionate feelings and have someone express those feelings to her. She knew, at the same time, that she'd never leave her husband for this man. She didn't even particularly like him—he was passive, not terribly interesting, professionally mediocre; he couldn't get his act together. She understood that it was never serious, but a reversion to her adolescent seductive acting out, making the boys fall for her. And in the background, she was dancing around Harry, shouting, "Look at me, look what I'm doing."

Alice was on a collision course with her partner, although he didn't know it. Something there would have popped sooner or later.

The pop came from another corner altogether. Leading his graduate seminar one morning, Harry suddenly couldn't think of what to say next. He tried to speak but no words came. By the end of the day, the family knew that Harry had suffered a mild stroke, and that although all indications were he'd eventually be fine, he was in for a slow and lengthy period of recovery.

A little over a year later, Harry was essentially back to normal and able to resume most of his teaching duties. But that was a year that changed the couple fit between Alice and Harry forever, and ultimately for better.

Here was a man who, throughout adulthood, had derived his primary sense of identity from his professional activities. Teaching, advising students, researching, writing, and publishing gave him his deepest satisfaction, and in that academic arena he was assertive, creative, generous, and successful. In his intimate relationships, with his wife and to some extent also with his children, however, Harry was not quite there most of the time.

The stroke altered not only the course of his days but the tenor of his thoughts as well. When he wasn't engaged in one of the therapy sessions necessary to regain his strength and control, Harry spent many quiet hours at home alone. In the early months of his recovery, he was often deeply depressed. With his identification of respected professor and scholar stripped away, he hardly knew where or how to locate husband and father, an aspect of life he'd taken seriously and responsibly but from which he drew little sense of self. For the first time, really, he thought about his wife and his children, how dear to him they were, and how little, oddly, he knew about them in some ways. He thought about how he couldn't imagine pulling through this now without Alice's care and support. Suddenly, he was deeply touched by and grateful for his family.

Toward the end of his recovery period, with his depression lifted and his control restored, Harry started to tell his wife all that—how much he appreciated her, how much he loved her, how he could see that probably a lot of the time he wasn't a hell of a lot of fun to live with. He told her that he wanted to do better, making up to her for past sins of omission, and wooing her again. He was telling Alice all the things she had wanted to hear.

And she had no idea what to do with them. She could hardly bear all that emoting from her once-distant partner! Alice was thrown off her rails, becoming alternately teary, agitated, or scared. In her ambivalent way of attaching, she'd always pushed and pulled at Harry, trying and usually failing to *get* something from him. Now that that something was offered, she was at a loss as to how to take it in.

That's the point at which Harry and Alice came for some counseling. Over many sessions, each proved to be insightful and adept at describing thoughts and feelings—what had attracted one to the other in the first place, what made them laugh, what values they shared, and how each "saw" the marriage from this midway point in its time. With the counselor steering matters along, they told each other what one would like more of and what one would like less of.

Ultimately, Harry and Alice got a great combination working. He was better able to demonstrate the love that had always been there; she could accept and take in his feelings without becoming overwhelmed by them. (She stopped the affairs, dropped the friendship with Harry's colleague, and elected not to tell her husband about past behaviors that would cause him pain and that she had no intention of repeating.) They went for and achieved a greatly more mature couple fit, one within which each partner felt better understood and more deeply content. The good in the relationship, and there was much good, could blossom. They felt, they said, like a couple of kids again.

If there's a moral to the story of Harry and Alice, it might be this: Watch out what you wish for, because you might get it.

If there's a message, it's this: When one partner changes, so must the other. With the inevitability of a mathematical equation, change on one side automatically alters the other. And change is seldom a bed of roses.

When couples come to us for counseling, one or the other will often say, "He just needs to stop doing XYZ; that's the problem." To which we often reply, "And when he stops doing XYZ, what will you have to complain about? Where will your anger be directed? How will you express the frustrations you obviously feel? When he changes, what shakes out for you after that?"

In other words, we start preparing these pairs for a possibly rocky road coming up. The bumps in the road may not jut up as suddenly, dramatically, and traumatically as they did for Harry and Alice, who because of one life event were instantly wrenched out of habitual ways of behaving. But any degree of disaffection, anger, unhappiness, or loneliness that eventually prompts one partner to wish and strive for something better is itself a trauma. It initiates a process that is never easy and sometimes painful.

We laid out at the beginning of *Couple Fits* our professional bias—that partners in a marriage or long-term love relationship should stick together, barring the presence of genuinely unacceptable behavior, such as physical abuse. A biblical commentary identifies adultery, private insult, and public humiliation as three essentially mortal assaults to the union. The point is that any actions by one or both partners that breach critical feelings necessary to the formation and life of an intimate relationship—basic trust, self-esteem, a sense of personal limits—may be damaging beyond the possibility of repair. When interactions have become punitive, destructive, critical, hostile, and negative; when the rules of intimacy continue to be violated; when partners find themselves unable to limit abusive behavior; and when private attempts to resolve such serious conflicts are not succeeding, that couple should consider obtaining professional help. Insights and guidance offered by a qualified and objective third party can be of immense value.

Most of the pairs we counsel, happily, are far from such dire straits. They want to stay together; they *should* stay together; and they pick up some good ideas and a few useful tools to make that happen. The essential attachment pattern, the "bones" of the couple, don't usually change without long-term, intensive professional treatment, and most relationships can't tolerate that kind of time and energy. Thankfully, most relationships don't require it.

What we see as counselors—and what we hope you have learned and will take away from *Couple Fits*—is that two individuals within a love relationship can make huge improvements in how they behave toward each other, and that is often quite sufficient. With those useful tools, they figure out how to forge a better connection, feel more satisfied, live together with a bit more ease, and sustain a greater degree of comfort. They can do that now, these men and women who once were so miserable that they'd drive around in their cars in the evening, dreading the moment of coming home.

So forge your own better fit with the tools you've learned here. Throughout this book we've referred to workable adjustments and temporary negotiations, those incremental changes that sweeten the day and then, in time, reshape the fit. Keep putting them into play, even when the payoff seems slow in coming, because many small steps—if you really want them to work—do ensure a long-term gain.

Add this element to the mix: Give your partner praise for his or her own successfully achieved workable adjustment or temporary negotiation.

Perhaps you've heard this rather cynical injunction: "Beat your children once a day. If you don't know the reason for it, they do." We would apply a more kindly version to the marital or love relationship: "Praise your partner regularly. If you don't know why such praise is deserved, your partner will."

When things are going well (or at least, better), and you're enjoying the improved atmosphere, you may simultaneously entertain one or more of the following thoughts:

He's doing what he should have been doing all along.
Finally, this guy gets the idea!
He's on his good behavior now, but how long is *this* going to last?
He managed to act like a normal human being for a change.
(And the old favorite:) I'm the one who got him to do this, so why give him credit for it?

All are, undoubtedly, valid thoughts. But here is where you should go the extra yard, bite the bullet if you must, and offer a little praise: I really appreciated the way you took care of that matter we talked about . . . the way you acted with the kids today . . . the way you were nice to my mother . . . the way you gave me a hug and a kiss when you came home from work.

A standard child-raising dictum says that a parent achieves better results from reenforcing the good behavior than from slapping down the bad. It works for love partners too.

Couple Fits outlines a good and psychologically sound method, one that enables you to see yourself and your partner without getting defensive, without feeling threatened or guilty. You're not doing anything bad or wrong and neither is your partner. You are how you are, brought in from elsewhere. First, defocus the blame. Then improve, in small ways, your manner of connecting. You'll increase your comfort level; you won't have to drive around half the night, but can go home and talk and go to sleep and wake up in a better place. When you change the small behaviors and find greater comfort, then ideally over time the feelings change too, and you can help your partner along, help both of you live together better.

This is what love has to do with it: Love will empower you. When the love is strong enough, action and empathy are possible. That kind of love carries with it sufficient idealism to enable you to give, forgive, adjust, and accommodate. That kind of love includes the trust each couple needs to work out their own rules of intimacy and reach a better, happier, more comfortable fit.

Index

Contact Information

Evelyn S. Cohen
The New York Institute for Psychological Change
180 East 79th St.
New York, NY 10021
212-348-1658
escohen@mindsring.com

Sheila A. Rogovin
35 Wisconsin Circle
Chevy Chase, MD 20815
301-951-1066
sarogovin@yahoo.com

Author Information

Evelyn S. Cohen, M.S., is a marriage and family therapist with the New York Institute for Psychological Change. She is frequently invited to address employees of such corporations as Salomon Brothers and Chase Manhattan.

Sheila A. Rogovin, Ph.D., is a psychotherapist in private practice in Chevy Chase, MD. She lives in Washington, D.C., with her husband, Stewart L. Aledort, M.D.